Standing at the Edge
by Rita J. Weber

Library of Congress Control Number: 2005900567

ISBN: 1-57579-304-0

First printing, February 2005
Second printing, July 2007

Contact Information:
Blind Trust, Inc
P.O. Box 90217
Sioux Falls, SD 57109-0217
e-mail: rita@blindtrustinc.com
website: www.blindtrustinc.com

Printed in the United States of America
PINE HILL PRESS
4000 West 57th Street
Sioux Falls, SD 57106

Dedication

To my husband, Karl,
for his help and support
And to our children
for the joy they bring me

Table of Contents

Acknowledgments

A special word of thanks and deep appreciation is given for the individuals who read over the manuscript and offered suggestions for its improvement. Alice Jones and Randy Hummel were gentle guides in taking me through the realities of editing. Each had a generosity of spirit as they assisted me in identifying areas for further work, while providing words of encouragement and hope. I will appreciate the work always.

A special thank you to the staff of Pine Hill Press for their expertise and skill in the publication process.

I also wish to give a word of appreciation for those family members and friends who offered words of encouragement and support during the process of this project. Those who told me to write and who bolstered me in times of doubt and discouragement have as much a share in this effort as I, for without their help, I could not have completed the work.

The greatest thanks goes to my husband, Karl, who told me I needed to write this book, and on whose prompting I finally sat down to do it. Much thanks and love I give to you and to our children.

Above all, I acknowledge the work of the Holy Spirit in inspiring and illuminating the everyday incidents of life to teach me what I needed to know to live life more fully. All glory and honor be given to my Lord, Jesus Christ, from whom all good things flow.

A Song and A Prayer? Introduction

It started in the spring of 2001. I was struggling to determine if the call to attend seminary was God's call or my own idea. I read the Scriptures. I lay prostrate on the floor praying and seeking God's will for me. This didn't make any sense to me. Here I was, forty-nine years old and almost totally blind. Why would God call me to attend seminary? And, what could He possibly do with me once I finished?

After weeks of feeling confused by what this was about, I rose early one morning. As I began to get ready for the day a song started to come out of my mouth. By the time I was finished dressing, there was a complete song that I could sing and repeat and remember. This had never happened to me before, and yet, here it was. I called to my husband and asked him to listen as I sang it for him. "Does that sound like a song to you?" I asked, tentatively.

"Well, yeah, it sounds like a song. It sounds like a prayer, actually."

I wasn't sure what that was all about, but the song—melody and harmony and lyric—was in my head. I went to the piano and tried to determine how to play it. It took several tries before I located the keys. It sounded like a song. Maybe I had heard it on the radio and it stuck in my head, I thought. I listened intently over the next weeks for the tune, but I never heard it. What could this be about? I really didn't know for sure, except that it spoke to me very clearly about the struggle I had been going through to discern God's will. And, its message, based on Proverbs 3:5-6, was clear. Apparently, I didn't need to understand why God was calling me to seminary. All I needed to do was to trust Him enough to obey.

I sang that song to myself many times during those weeks and months before starting classes in the fall of 2001. It gave me assurance like nothing else had. I knew that I was doing what I was called to do. Even though my finances couldn't handle the expensive tuition and my husband was opposed to the idea, I knew that I had to do it, no matter what the cost.

This book is written to offer insights into living in dependence on God. The struggles of life can easily send us scrambling to make sense of our experiences. The challenge of coming to terms with my vision loss is only part of what *Standing At The Edge* is about.

Each one of us, whether dealing with a disability or not, is limited in our capacity to live life fully. It is impossible to be all that we were created to be, unless we turn over all that we are, all we have been, and all we will become into God's care. That is how God intended things to be. Our attempts to shortchange that process and to rely on our own abilities, our finite selves, dooms us to a life that falls short of what might have been—no matter how successful we may appear to be by this world's standards.

Included amid the stories and insights that I share in this book, I have included the lyrics to several of the songs that I have written over the past 3 years. These writings have come to me in various ways—some were fully formed when they showed up in my thoughts, others were ideas that required much time and development before they were fully revealed to me.

Whichever way they came—while walking on the treadmill, or in a burst of inspiration while sitting on a beach—the truth about each of them is that they were not my creations. Oh, I wrote them and the melodies to which they are sung, but the Holy Spirit is responsible for them. I can't write songs. I tried that in the past with abysmal results.

These songs are intentionally scripture-based. The songs of the past—those by Luther, the Wesleys, Fanny J. Crosby—had a clear theological message. The songs of the past were not merely to move people emotionally; they were also for the intent and purpose of teaching correct theology.

The songs I have been given are for that purpose as well. They may be used in worship, but they are not the repetitive words of the worship choruses that are found in many of today's popular worship lyrics.

As you read the pages that follow, I encourage you to allow God's Spirit to speak through them. His message to us is clear in the Scriptures. Humanly speaking, we cannot ever do or be what we need to be in this lifetime, in spite of our best efforts. But God, (Praise His Name!) is merciful and full of grace. He makes us righteous by his perfection, not our own. As Christ covers us, our God sees us as holy and perfect.

That is the reason we have hope in this world so filled with corruption and evil. In spite of all that we see, Christ has already claimed victory over all the evil of this world. It is a done deal. We can place our faith in that promise. We can fully rest in the true and risen Lord Jesus Christ. We can live in a place of complete peace and confidence when we receive the gift of faith. God gives us faith. We only need to receive his gift!

Trust In The Lord

Words and music by Rita Weber
Copyright © 2001 by Rita Weber

Refrain
Trust in the Lord with all your heart
And do not lean on your own understanding.
In all your ways acknowledge him
And he'll direct your paths.

When my life is filled with trouble
And I don't know what to do,
I just fall upon my knees and cry to God.
There, he sees me with compassion
And he takes me to his word.
He reminds me that his promises are true.

To Refrain

When it seems that I'm inadequate
to rise up to the task,
I know God's grace will suffice for what I lack.
For, it's when I'm at my weakest
That the Lord is at his best.
He will help me, all I have to do is ask.

To Refrain

If it feels your heart is breaking over precious things you've lost,
Just remember that the Lord is by your side.
He has come to bring new meaning,
To bring joy in place of pain.
You can leave your heavy burden at the cross.

To Refrain

"Rawkin' and Sangin'"

Henry wasn't like anyone else I ever knew. He looked like the Colonel on the Kentucky Fried Chicken barrels—minus the white suit and the goatee—and he had a drawl that betrayed his roots in the Kentucky hills. His bulbous nose and rotund belly were cause for study by this curious little girl who didn't realize that others might notice her stare.

His wife was as far to the other end of the continuum as could be from his own colorful character. She moved around the house in a quiet, depressed state. Oh, she smiled on occasion, but more often she was frowning and looking as though something was bothering her.

Their home was small, and located on the other side of the river. My family and I had to cross the bridge and go around the curve to get to the little wooden house with a small front porch that was illuminated in the evenings by one of those bug-repellent, yellow lights. The house was built a couple hundred feet from the bank of the slow part of the river and it was butted up against the tree-filled bluff that rose up high above it. The back window of the house gave no view save the side of the steep embankment. Inside the little kitchen, a door opened to a storage cave lined with shelves where all their perishables could be stored at a suitable temperature year round. Out in the side yard, a large pole stood completely covered in clamshells, dark side against the post, revealing the colorful "mother-of-pearl" in every direction.

Childless, the couple always kept caramels in the candy jar and a welcoming heart for us—a brood of noisy, unruly kids. Our visits seemed to brighten their spirits a bit. Henry and Erma were warm to us, in spite of their cantankerous attitude to one another.

Henry would settle into one of his green metal lawn chairs and begin to talk with my brothers and sisters and me, slowly at first, then with growing enthusiasm and drama as he shared stories of the past. Whether they were true or not, I couldn't say, but, he could make a big story out of very little. It provided a good bit of entertainment for us whether listening to Henry in the original, or my brother Curt's exquisite imitation later.

"Why, I remember that winter when I was laid up with that bad ankle," Henry began, reminiscing with me when I was grown. He had told his recollections many times, but it was always fun to hear him say it, as if for the first time. "You and Lyn were no bigger than this." (At this point, he held out his hand about seventeen inches from the floor.) "And you two would get up in that rawkin' chair, and you'd rawk and sing "Jesus Loves Me" over and over for all you was worth."

I can't remember much about this particular winter that Henry recalled. The couple's house didn't seem to have many furnishings. Henry's bed, a little twin-sized cot, sat in the middle of the living room. In front of the south window next to the bed, was the big old carved rocking chair and sitting next to it, the large wooden buffet that held the glass candy jar. The chair was big enough to accommodate Lynn and I side-by-side with our feet sticking straight out off the front of it.

He was right, we did love to sing. "Jesus Loves Me" was one of the songs that I can't remember learning. I think I knew it before I could talk!

Remembering that song and how many hundreds of times I had sung it over the years, not only for Henry, but also just for singing's sake, I began to think about how I imagined God when I was a little girl. It seemed I thought a great deal about being weak and God being strong. I thought about knowing that God loved me just because the Bible told me so. I didn't know all I wanted to know about God, but I knew that much—God loved me.

A year or so ago, I was in the final stretch of seminary. I had been studying Theology and reading and praying for insights. The more I learned, though, the more I started to realize that I didn't know much more about God now than I had when I was a kid. There were so many things that I just couldn't fully grasp. There was so much that was still a mystery to me. I realized that, after all this seminary training, the only thing I knew for certain was that God loved me. That old song that my sister and I sang for Henry had been greater wisdom than I could have ever grasped as a child. *Jesus loves me…*

This I Know

Words and music by Rita Weber
Copyright © 2003 by Rita Weber

When I was only a child, I loved to sing for you.
And, with my simple words, I told you that I love you.
I didn't understand all the words I sang,
Like mercy and grace.
I just thanked you, Lord, for dying in my place.

I didn't understand how you were God and man,
Or how a God so big could fit inside a baby.
I only knew you came because you love me.
Each day, you love me just the same.

Why did you leave heaven to die upon a tree?
Why did you give up your life to give new life to me?
I couldn't understand it, how you could love me so.
'Jesus loves me. This I know.'

Now, many years have passed
Since I lived in those childhood days.
And, yet I wonder how much things have really changed.
I still don't understand the wonders of your mercy and grace.
And, I never will until I see your face.

I still don't understand your great salvation plan,
the blessed Trinity, or resurrection mysteries.
I only know you came because you loved us,
So much you called us, 'Children of God.'

Why did you leave glory to die upon a tree?
Why did you lay down your life for sinful souls like me?
I still can't comprehend it, this debt of love I owe.
'Jesus loves me. This I know."

Highways and Byways *Chapter 2*

Music had been part of our family life always. Dad played a guitar. He taught my sister, Bonnie, to play a few chords on the piano, and before long the two of them were playing and singing sacred songs in church.

One Saturday afternoon, he brought home instruments bought second-hand from a place in the city. Soon, Gary was playing mandolin, Curt was on the Hawaiian guitar, and Danny played a banjo. The five of them sounded great together.

By the time I was five, Dad had decided that Lynn and I should begin to sing along. He and Bonnie told me to listen as they sang the song, "Suppertime." It took a few tries, but, at last, it clicked! There was a harmony part as clear as could be.

With Lynn singing melody and me singing alto, we began to learn to sing together. It didn't all come easy, but we had fun singing along with the family. Mom would sit and listen, holding our youngest sister, Susie.

It was a sacrifice for Mom and Dad to buy these used instruments. They hardly had enough to buy the necessities of life, but Dad felt strongly that we were supposed to be in a music ministry. He had dreams that one day the whole family would travel around singing and playing.

It didn't turn out exactly as he planned. He was not a marketing sort of person. One day, after a friend of Dad's dropped by for a visit, things changed. Lenny and his cousin, Ernest, had been traveling around to area towns setting up a microphone on Friday or Saturday nights right on Main Street. They would pass out tracts and Ernest would preach. The idea of having music to draw people in to listen seemed like a great idea to both Dad and Lenny.

Things were different in the Midwest in the 1950's than they are today. Stores weren't open twenty-four hours a day, seven days a week. The streets were rolled up by 5:00 p.m. except for one night—a Friday or Saturday, depending on the town. Then, everyone came to town to do their shopping. The stores were open until 9 o'clock that night, and most towns had a cash drawing that would keep people around for the evening. It was a great time to shop and socialize.

Our family would be all dressed up on that night in our one good Sunday outfit. Our hair was washed and combed and braided or put in a ponytail. Then, we were off!

It seemed that we went hundreds of miles on those trips. When we arrived in town, the Gordon cousins, or one of the other members of the ministry team, would go into the local bar and pay anyone who was willing to move their car from in front of the place to get the prime parking spot. After that was accomplished, they would get permission to plug in our sound system into an outlet in the bar. When all that was done, Ernest would take his place in front of the microphone, wearing his bolo tie, his horn-rimmed glasses and a large straw hat. His words still ring in my mind, "We are commanded by Jesus to go out into the highways and the byways and compel them to come in."

I didn't understand exactly what that meant, or the text in Luke he referred to, but the phrase was as predictable a part of these nights as the 9 o'clock whistle blowing. We would get ready to do our part.

At age five and seven, Lynn and I made our debut. We didn't know what to expect, but we didn't have much choice. We stood up to sing when Ernest announced our song. Kneecaps quivering, we sang our best. Then, we hurried back to the rear of the car. Our part was over!

People were kind most of the time, considering that we were in competition with the bar's booming jukebox! Some would come up to us and tell us to keep on singing for the Lord. There was ridicule by others. It was probably more difficult for my older brothers and sister. They weren't as naïve as Lynn and I were back then.

We spent most weekends of the summer going out on these "street meetings." As the family grew up, it was Lynn and I who went off with the Gordons or other friends of our father, to provide the music.

Eventually, Susie, our younger sister, began to sing a third, higher part with us. We sang for several years as an acapella trio.

Did anyone ever find Christ in all those years? It's hard to say. But, maybe one day we will meet a person in heaven who found the Lord because of one of those meetings. It is God that saves, not us.

But You Don't Have To

Words and music by Rita Weber
Copyright © 2001 by Rita Weber

Lonely people, empty lives—
All of them reaching out to find something to fill them.
Some are angry, some confused.
I want so much to help them all, but I can't.

But you don't have to, says the Lord.
I am the one who came to heal the broken-hearted.
Be my vessel, my hands and feet.
All of the things that you would do,
let it be my Spirit's work through you.
Bring my love to all you meet.

I am hope for the hopeless,
I am sight for the blind.
I am the Bread of Life who fills all those who hunger.
I am rest for the weary.
I am peace for those in fear.
I have come to save the world—so you don't have to.

Lord, you know me.
You see my heart.
You know how much I long to be
Your faithful servant.
But, I stumble and I fall.
I want to do as you would do, but I can't.

But you don't have to, says the Lord.
I am the one who came to give my gift of mercy.
You be holy, for I am holy.
It is a gift I give to you,
Not earned by anything you do.
Only by faith do you receive.

I am God who makes you righteous.
I am God who sets you free.
I am God who blots out
All of your offenses.
I am God who has given you my gift of eternal life.
I chose to die for all your sins—so you don't have to.

Pathways In Paradise

The "street meeting" years occurred during our time at the river, just down the gravel and across the bridge from Henry's place. It is home in my mind, when I think about home.

The place was known as "Albright's Mill." The mill that it was named for had burned down, leaving just a couple of cement wall remains to mark its location. It wasn't good for anything except burning our trash.

There was a little general store that still had wooden barrels full of crackers and a large spool of string hanging over the cash register to tie around paper wrapped packages. The store had closed earlier that year and Jessie, its proprietor, lived behind it in a nicely kept apartment at the back of the store. Her outdoor pump was our only source of water when we first moved in.

The old creamery that had been a busy place in previous days stood across the road, in total disrepair, until Bob Devlin covered a part of the roof and occupied one end of it.

Our house stood up on the hill next to the store. It was a small, white, wood-frame house that had served Albright's as the Feed Store in former times. It wasn't much of a house, but it had huge grape vines that hung full on its south side. There birds would gather and sing.

The huge, old chain that had served to tie up wagons and horses still hung between the thick fence posts that rimmed the east of our property. And, four huge Cottonwood trees, so big that even grown-ups couldn't get their arms around them towered over the house, rustling in the slightest breeze.

The buildings were located around a figure-8 gravel drive that had been well traveled in the past. The grass in the middle of the larger circle made a perfect infield for our blossoming athletic efforts. The smaller circle held a row of mailboxes This was home.

The Crow River that curled around through the pasture that was on our land was deep in parts and shallow in others. The old dam that had been built in the '30's had broken down during a past flood, its stones and the water flowing over them creating a beautiful white water rapid there in the middle of the river.

The flooding had left behind a white-sugar sand beach that curved along the river at the shallow part. It was great swimming for swimmers who were just learning to swim. And, swim, we did! Morning, noon, and night, we swam in the river, unsupervised, except for one another.

In the winter we enjoyed ice skating and sledding and fishing and in the summer–swimming, fishing, and hiking. What more could a child want? It was paradise!

One of our greatest pleasures was on Sunday afternoons. Mom and Dad always took a nap on Sundays. We didn't have to nap, if we didn't want to, but we had to be quiet!

Sometimes, our oldest brother, Gary, would take us for a hike in the woods. We would walk down the gravel, across the bridge, through the barbed wire fence, and into the neighbor's pasture that was on the opposite side of the river from our own land. We had to watch out for "cow pies," as we made our way over the flat part of the pasture. Our ascent was made up a narrow path that climbed up the side of a steep hill. It took us to the top of a bluff that stood high over the Crow River below. Many places became narrow, and we had to stay on the path and not get too close to the edge.

"Watch out," Gary would warn. "You never know where the bank has eroded out from beneath the top of the hill. If you get too close to the edge, you might break through and fall down the bluff."

Whether the peril was truly that real, or whether it was just to keep us in line–it worked. We walked along ever so carefully, making sure not to go too close to impending doom just feet away.

As we walked along the bluff that overlooked the part of the river we used for swimming, we would stop and look at the rapids from this lofty vantage point. It all looked different from way up here. The yellow colored bluff that held scores of small holes made by swallows who nested in its bank was positioned below us now. Instead of watching the birds high overhead, we watched from above as they flew swiftly through the air below us, beneath the grassy pastureland we traveled.

Gary would let us look for a while, then he'd say, "Let's get going."

The well-worn parts of the path vanished. We would still walk in single file behind our brother. He was tall and kept the pace just fast enough so we had to keep moving if we didn't want to be lost out in this unfamiliar wilderness.

The journey lasted for hours, literally. We walked on and on, uncertain of our location. Then, all of a sudden, we would come up to the road that drove past Albright's or come into a clearing where things looked familiar.

It was such an adventure, not knowing for sure where we were or where we were going. We were completely dependent on Gary and his ability to know those things.

We were cautious never to lose sight of him. Part of what made the walks so exciting was that we were totally lost in our own minds, even though Gary always knew precisely where we were. We trusted him!

Eye Has Never Seen

Words and music by Rita Weber
Copyright © 2003 by Rita Weber

Jesus, let me be your faithful witness,
So that all I am brings glory to your Name.
Lord, by your Spirit, help me proclaim your love and grace.
Let me be your witness 'til I see you face-to-face.

I heard Jesus call my name.
He whispered, "Come follow.
Leave your earthly cares behind. Surrender to my will.
Take my yoke upon you, for my yoke is easy.
I'll be right there with you
As you bear my Light."
"Eye has never seen, ear has never heard,
All the things prepared for those who love me.
If you'll take my hand,
I'll lead you to heights you've never dreamed of.
Take up your cross. Follow me."

Life In Eden Chapter 4

A large, red barn that stood past Jessie's store and was connected to our house by a well-worn path was included in our rental property in Albright's. It was not in great condition, but it was where Cherry and Kappy and Lulabelle lived. These milk cows provided the fresh, raw milk for our family of nine. They also offered opportunities for many practical lessons in living life.

One lovely summer evening, we were getting ready to go to town to attend our weekly Bible study. Just as we were about to leave, someone came running in the house. Lulabelle had fallen into the mud of the river and couldn't get out. A fence must have broken.

"Stay in the house!" Mom warned, as she and my brothers went down to see what could be done to help Dad.

Lynn, Susie, and I positioned ourselves in the front window in the living room. We set our gaze through the screen, past the cottonwoods, over the log chain fence, across the figure-8 gravel road and saw the cow. Her "bellaring" could be heard echoing off the high bluffs. She must have been nearly as scared as we were. The bottom of the river where she had become mired was an area of backwater that stood still and had no current. The bottom was so mucky, it was a goo that worked like quick sand. The more Lulabelle struggled, the more she sank down into the mire.

It was no use. There was no way to get the cow out without extraordinary help. Mom called the people at church to tell them our dilemma. There was no way we could leave the cow and go to church.

"We'll just come out and have Bible study at your house, after we get the cow out of the river!" the pastor offered.

Soon help arrived on the scene. A tractor had to be hooked up to chains, the chains had to be put around the cow, and slowly they pulled her free from the mucky river bottom that held her captive.

It was such an exciting thing to see from our front window perch. We cared about Lulabelle. When we saw her freed at last, we who were watching from the house let out a cheer. She had been saved!

That night's Bible study seemed to be hand made by Lulabelle's dire straits of the early evening. The illustration of our lives and our times when we are slipping down further and further into the miry clay of sinfulness seemed an illustration that could not be passed up. Lulabelle couldn't save herself. Neither could we. We need to call for help, too. Then God comes and pulls us up out of that place that looked as though it would surely claim our life, had we not been pulled to safety. This lesson seared into my memory forever.

My memory also recalls the day when Mom looked out the kitchen window and cried out in horror, "The cows are in the corn!"

The significance of this discovery was lost on me. What was the big deal if they ate a little of the corn, I wondered? There is plenty of corn out there.

I had no idea the terrible problem that the cows would face that day. Their digestive system couldn't handle that corn. Their bellies began to swell as the gas formed in them, only hours after they had eaten. Fortunately, Mom had seen them before they had eaten much, so all they suffered was a painful belly and the most incredible diarrhea. They could have died, Mom told us later. They like the taste of the corn, but it isn't good for them! The cows weren't smart enough to know any better.

At the far end of the barn, there was a small covered shed that housed the hogs. They were interesting to watch, rooting around in the mud and snorting. Sometimes Mom would send me out to throw food scraps to them. They scrambled over to where the tasty treats were, pushing and shoving each other. Each of them was interested only in its own needs.

Around the barn, Dad grew huge vegetable gardens. We had plenty of opportunities for weed pulling and harvesting. When it was time to harvest the potatoes, Dad would dig up the potatoes with a small plow pulled behind the tractor. All of us would walk along behind, pulling the little potatoes out of the ground and brushing off the dirt. They were a staple in our diet. We kept them in a huge mountain in the cellar of the house. The crop would last most of the winter.

I loved living with all the animals and watching the plants grow from seeds into food. Our lives were simple. We had very few toys to play with, but it didn't seem important. There were no children around to compare our standard of material possessions with, so there was no awareness of deprivation.

During a summer drive recently, my older brother and sister took me around the countryside to see the various places that our father lived as a child. He moved several times, but as we drove, I couldn't help noticing that all of the houses were along the Crow River. He had told me about playing down by the river as a kid. Now it became evident that the river had been a big part of life for him.

In the last years of his life, he bought a piece of property and put his home on it where he and Mom lived for many years. To no one's surprise, it was along the Crow River.

Living By The River

Words and music by Rita Weber
Copyright © 2004 by Rita Weber

There were never trees that looked so green
Or stood so tall.
There were never birds that sang so sweet
As the ones in my childhood on the banks of the Crow.
I thought that living by the river was paradise.

Refrain
Paradise! Paradise!
There's no place on earth where life could be so sweet.
Splashing in the water, basking in the sun.
For children, living by the river was paradise.

The little house we lived in wasn't really much to see,
But our Daddy shared this secret there
With my family and me.
Though we might search the whole world over
There was nothing we would find
Worth more than living by the river in Paradise.

To Refrain

Daddy's life wasn't easy, his Papa died so young.
He had to live in many places as he grew.
But, he was always by the river,
where he'd run when work was through.
For Daddy, living by the river was paradise.

To Refrain

Now our Daddy's gone to glory.
All his work on earth is through.
But there's one thing that I know beyond a doubt—
His new home is by the River
Flowing from the Throne of God.
Now Daddy's living by the River in Paradise.

Paradise! Paradise!
There's no place on earth where life could be so sweet.
Splashing in the water, Basking in the Light of God the Son.
God's children living by the River in Paradise!

Hiding and Seeking *Chapter 5*

It was while I lived there in the paradise of Albright's that many important things happened–significant things. Maybe it was because I was five–nearly six–when we moved there, or maybe it was because it was the place I lived longest as a child.

I learned to tie my shoelaces there, I learned to read there, and to write, and to do arithmetic. I went up to the altar in church and asked Jesus to come into my heart when we lived there. And I learned how to ride a bike!

One night in early September, I hit a milestone. I was big enough so I could play outside in the dark with the "big kids." There I was with all those cousins and my older brother and sister playing "Hide-and-Seek." I felt very grown up. However, something strange happened there that night.

I was "It." I sat on the cement steps and counted to 100 by tens, since I couldn't count to 100 yet. Then, I stood up after reaching the final digit and called out my warning, "Here I come. Ready or not. No goal stickers!"

I charged forward to seek out my prey. I searched the bushes and the best hiding places, but I couldn't find anyone. Suddenly, I heard someone run past me–first one and then another, and another until everyone had made it to the goal safely. I had heard them running, but I couldn't see them. It was my turn again. Next time I would find them!

But, I didn't find them. Several times I was "It," but I never found anyone.

This was puzzling to me. Maybe this was one of those things that I hadn't learned yet, like multiplication. My sister would know. She could teach me to see in the dark.

I waited to ask Lynn about the special trick to seeing in the dark until the next day. But, when I asked her, she looked at me with a strange look and said, "What do you mean, 'How do you see in the dark?' You just open your eyes and look!" she exclaimed, widening her eyes as big as she could.

Oh-oh! I knew that there must be something wrong with me. Mom had told me once about another child who had trouble understanding things the way other children did. She said that some children were born that way and that they just needed extra help to learn. Did that explain what I had just experienced? I decided that I must be mentally slow and that was the reason I couldn't figure out how to see. I didn't know how, but I was sure that I needed to keep that a secret if I could.

It was a long time (at least several days!) before I found the courage to tell my mother. She was busy sweeping the floor. I talked and twirled around the kitchen and casually said, "When I was playing 'Hide-and-Seek' in the dark I couldn't see anybody."

Mom stopped sweeping and looked thoughtful for a minute. Then she gave me an answer to my confusion that was very helpful to me. She said, "Hm-m. You must have 'night-blindness' like your brother, Gary." We chatted about that a little while, and then she went back to her sweeping.

That was an important answer she gave me, because in my five-year-old year-old mind, the answer was interpreted like this—*some people have brown eyes. I have blue. Some people can see in the dark. I have night-blindness.*

Although that was a faulty understanding, it made me feel normal. I was a normal kid who had night-blindness. That was all I knew for a long, long time.

Growing older and having more time with friends, it was only a matter of time until I realized that no one else in the world had ever even heard of "night-blindness." They looked at me strangely, and I knew that this was one of those little secrets that I needed to keep quiet about. I worked hard never to let anyone know about my flawed sight.

One of the greatest challenges to my maintaining the illusion of normalcy was in Mr. Boyle's tenth-grade Chemistry class. We were taking a test that required use of the Periodic Table. I squinted from my front row seat, but it was no use. I would never be able to read the numbers on that chart.

Reluctantly, I went up to Mr. Boyle and told him about my dilemma. Could I use the Table in the back of the book, I whispered discreetly.

"Oh, no! I have just the thing for you."

He disappeared around the corner into a storage area behind the desk, and victoriously emerged with a small monocular device. "Here you go!" he crowed triumphantly.

It was humiliating, but I needed to pass the test. Sensitivity training and accommodations were not part of teacher training, apparently.

I made it through, turned in the test and fled to my next class. I tried to tell myself that it wasn't that bad. At least I had been able to read the numbers.

Just as I had nearly succeeded at convincing myself of that, my "friend" Bob came up, laughing. "You sure looked ridiculous with that stupid eyeglass thing!"

Thank you, Bob.

My vision was getting worse. Glasses were changed, but I never could see the board quite like I should. I paid close attention to the movements of the teacher's hand as he/she wrote and, most of the time, I could figure out what had been written. I was not going to let anyone know how little I saw. I could pretend that I could see, or so I thought.

Dating brought many opportunities to creatively hide my poor vision. I had many little strategies to find out where the Ladies' room was, or to order off a menu without seeing it, but one night, there was no way to overcome the obstacle that I encountered.

My date and I were attending a special football game at his big-city high school. He was returning for a homecoming event as an alumnus, and he invited me to go along. It was a night that hadn't gone all that well from the beginning. I had dressed all wrong, my hair wouldn't cooperate—that sort of thing. We were sitting in the stands of a huge stadium. It was so different from my own little high school games, where the spectators lined up behind a wire fence strung along the sidelines. I felt very much like the country bumpkin.

When the game was over, we walked out to the parking lot. I had done well going in to the place, because I was walking toward the light. But, as I walked into the darkness, a cement barrier in the parking lot eluded me. I tripped and fell hard on the asphalt. My hands and knees stung almost as much as my eyes with tears of humiliation. My date looked and saw me there on the ground. He came over, but not to help me up. He said under his breath, *"Get up! You're embarrassing me!"*

Now I clearly see that he was inconsiderate and I should never have given him the opportunity to see me again, but at the time, I saw *me* as the problem. I tried to explain that I had night-blindness when we were safely in the car, but things were never the same between us.

Fortunately, a year later I met the man who is now my husband. I told him about my little problem with seeing in the dark. He seemed curious, but not incapable of understanding and acceptance.

A year after we met, we were married. He was a teacher. I was a nurse. We settled into a little 3-bedroom ranch and knew that we were on our way to the fulfillment of all our dreams!

When my twenty-first birthday came two weeks after we married, I went to change my name on my Driver's License and renew it all at the same time. It wasn't surprising to me when I failed the eye test. After all, I hadn't passed it when I took it at age sixteen either. I knew I would need to go and have a doctor write a permission slip so I could drive anyway. I had expected that. Something I didn't expect was about to occur.

As a provided benefit for my work as a nurse, I was able to receive free medical care at the world-famous clinic in town. I sat down in the Ophthalmology Department and waited for my name to be called. Soon, I was inside going through the routine of an eye test I had been through many times before. It became clear that something had turned a corner. We were no longer doing the usual. He ran tests, took an extensive family history, asked about my night-blindness and my brother, Gary. Finally, he sat down face-to-face and told me what he had discovered. It wasn't simply a case of night-blindness or poor, incorrectable close up vision. Those were only symptoms of a much bigger problem. I was going blind!

I sat there, numbed by the news. He called it Retinitis Pigmentosa. It was genetic, he said, with no treatment and no cure. There was no way to know for sure how long my vision would last, but the retinas of my eyes would continue to deteriorate until I was unable to see.

"Are you all right?" he asked with a gentle and empathetic tone.

I assured him how fine I was and stumbled out of that office, pupils dilated, to make my way back home. The elevator door opened and I stepped inside. *Funny*, I thought, aware of the others in the elevator that day, *they don't realize that I'm going blind. They think I'm normal.* As we rode in silence, they may have been dealing with the world crashing around them, too.

It was dusk as I arrived at the parking ramp. My dilated pupils and my night-blindness were potentially a deadly combination. Somehow, I made it home.

By the time I arrived there, I had already moved from the shock and numbness of my recent diagnosis, and was well into denial. My husband, concerned that I was home so late, met me at the door.

I couldn't tell him. He hadn't bargained for this when we took our vows two weeks earlier. We had planned many things for our "happily ever after," but not one of them included that I would be blind.

Blindness seemed like it would be something off in the far distant future. That is how I presented it to my husband, Karl. "I am losing my eyesight, and if I live to be an old woman, I probably won't be able to see any more." That was as much of the truth as I could share.

My vision was deteriorating rapidly. I asked for a reassignment at work. It was becoming more and more difficult to feel safe in performing my duties as a floor nurse. I woke up at night, heart pounding, after nightmares that my patients had died in the night, and I had not seen it. I didn't want to pass medications anymore. What if I made a fatal error? I met with my supervisor.

"We can't keep you on if you can't perform the duties you were hired to do. The role that you were hired for requires that you pass medications," she said. "You could transfer to the operating room. There you wouldn't have to pass meds."

I thanked God. Not only could I stop passing meds, I had all day shifts, with no more weekends or holidays.

What seemed like the perfect solution soon revealed a problem. For many weeks I studied the specialized skills for assisting in by-pass surgery, preparing to work with the cardio-thoracic surgeons. "Today, Rita, you will come up and assist the doctor yourself," my trainer informed me.

Nervously, I stood in place beside the surgeon, a kindly fellow, known worldwide for his skills. It seemed so amazing to be here, handing him forceps, providing the tools necessary to perform this life-saving operation.

Then it happened. He handed me a forceps with a needle but the suture was gone. I was about to put it back in its place on the tray.

"No, you need to rethread it," my trainer whispered, her gloved hand on mine and looking at me over her surgical mask.

Carefully, I put the suture up to the eye of the curved needle and pushed. It didn't go through. I tried again. The same thing happened.

"You're just nervous. You'll get it with practice," assurance came from across the operating table, as she picked up the needle and slipped the suture into the little hole with ease. "You can get the next one," she said.

In between the needs of the surgeon, I worked on another, but I could not thread it. For the next days I practiced. I tried. I could not thread the needles.

The supervisor looked over her glasses at me. There was no smile on her face. There was no compassion in her voice. She was cold as I pled my case.

"You were hired to assist the doctor, not to be a circulating nurse. If you can't do the job, you can't stay. I'm sorry you can't see, but that is not my problem."

She did concede that I could stay until my first baby was to be born, a few months later. That would be the end of my work. I wouldn't be a nurse in the O.R. anymore.

Within three years of diagnosis, I had to quit my nursing career. I had to surrender my Driver's License. I had to begin working with Rehabilitation Services to the Blind.

My husband, Karl, hadn't bargained for all this. Though we took our vows seriously, there was no way he could have anticipated that his promise to be there "in sickness and in health" was going to be put to the test in such a short time. I worried about Karl and our future. What if he didn't want to stay?

A couple years ago, as I thought about the great gift of my marriage, I sat down at the piano. My husband had been given a challenge. Our marriage commitment had been put to the test. Now, thirty years later, those challenges had brought us together in ways that few couples are brought together. As I placed my hands on the keys, this song emerged. My husband read the words I wrote.

"This sounds like a love song," he said.

"It *is* a love song," I answered.

When Love has Lasted

Words and music by Rita Weber
Copyright © 2002 by Rita Weber

When love has lasted for a lifetime,
When two hearts joined have been made one,
The joys and tears, that have come throughout the years,
Have formed a bond that makes this love so strong.

We come today to mark this anniversary—
To celebrate this covenantal love.
The friends and family here
All join these two, so dear,
In giving thanks and praise to God above.

God has blessed this holy union
With grace and strength for each new day.
The years may fade, but not the promises they've made.
There hearts go on repeating, "I still do!"

Who Am I, Anyway?

Chapter 6

It was a long time before I was able to let go of my denial and come to terms with the reality of my vision loss. I put on a smile and told everyone who asked that I was doing fine.

In truth, I would go down to my laundry room, turn on the washer and dryer, shut the door and cry my eyes out. I felt so bad for me and for my husband and for my kids.

It wasn't fair! There were other people in this world who didn't need to see as much as I did! I have children to care for and a career that I wanted to pursue. Why God?

Even now, it is hard to see all the things that brought me to a healthier place. I'm sure I had people praying for me. I tried to find answers to the reason for my calamity by reading Scripture and through prayer. I needed answers.

I returned to school. Work may not have been as important to me if I hadn't been going blind. Somehow, I needed to feel that I had worth. I didn't know who I was anymore. I didn't seem to fit with people who were blind, but I didn't fit with people who could see either. The only thing I was good at was school, it seemed. I desperately needed to feel capable at something.

After I received my degree in Social Work, I started working in a long-term care facility. That was a place where I discovered something important that I had never understood before.

Mom had quoted many Scripture passages as we grew up. The one that I was about to get—finally—was, "We know that all things work together for good for those who love God, who are called according to his purpose." (Romans 8:28,NRSV). Mom told us that the verse says "*All* things," not just good things. Even bad things work to our good.

Part of my role was to meet new residents and take a Social History for the chart. I would walk in with my white cane, sit down and visit, and then go on about my business. Then something happened. Residents started to give me feedback about the impact of my visit on them.

The comments usually went something like this: "I came here from the hospital so discouraged, certain that I would never be able to have a good life again. Then you came in with a white cane, working and happy, and then I knew—if you can do it, I can do it!"

Don't get me wrong. This was nothing special that I was doing. I was just living life. But, somehow, God was using my blindness as a tool for healing or hope for others. It became clearer to me each day that, in my own brokenness, the Light of Christ was showing through to those people who were in their own place of darkness.

In II Corinthians 4, Paul writes about earthen vessels. Now these earthen vessels were as common and cheap and expendable as Styrofoam is for us today. People used them for storing anything from jewelry to parchments to food. The only drawback was that they broke easily and once broken, they could not be repaired.

In the passage in chapter 4, it says that we are like these earthen vessels. What is inside us is the treasure that is the Light of Christ. The great difference is that, when we, as followers of Christ, are put under pressure or knocked down, we are not destroyed. That is so the Light that we carry can show out into this world and reveal the power that is God!

We may not even be aware that this is the case in our own experience, yet people around us are helped because of those places in our lives where we have breaks and cracks.

If you took a Styrofoam cup and drew on it the significant struggles you have had in your life, making a hole in the cup for the times when you felt broken, then you could shine a flashlight up underneath it and see what Paul was talking about. The light can't help but come through.

You know it is true from your own experience. We know of people who have lost a child, who reach out to others who lose a child, or a person who has recovered from cancer who reaches out in a special way to others who have been given that diagnosis. It is not our own light and power that makes the difference for others—it is God's!

I recall one dear lady who made a difference for me. She was new in the facility and I made my way into her room. Her daughter explained to me that her mother, a sweet, little, ninety-something, was not able to hear. She was wearing a small box around her neck and her daughter told me I would need to speak directly into it. Not only could she not hear, she was also totally blind.

I picked up the box and began to speak. "Hello, Myrtle. Your daughter tells me that you have trouble hearing. Are you able to hear my voice right now?" I asked her.

"Yes," the woman answered, smiling. " My daughter's right. I can't hear and I can't see, *but*, " she paused for emphasis, "I sleep *great*!"

How could I fail to be encouraged by an attitude like that one? It was a powerful model of how to make the best out of difficult circumstances.

Earthen Vessels

Words and music by Rita Weber
Copyright © 2002 by Rita Weber

Earthen Vessels, so easily broken,
Hold a treasure for all to see.
For the Light of Christ, which has shown in our hearts
Is the Light for all the world.

Earthen Vessels are often afflicted.
Though struck down, we are not destroyed.
So the world may know of the extraordinary power of God
Revealed in us.

Don't lose heart in the times of your affliction.
On the inside, God renews us day by day.
All the things that we see are only temporary things,
But the things that we can't see are eternal!

No Way

It has been twenty-six years since I received the letter. It came from the doctor's office and I knew it contained information regarding my latest eye test. It explained in a formal way that I now met the criteria, under codified law such-and-such, and that I was formally being declared, "legally blind." The letter went on to say that I was now entitled to all the "benefits" provided by the state.

Laughter welled up inside me. I began to ridicule this insensitive doctor and the letter he had just sent. I thought, *what sort of benefits would you be willing to take in exchange for your vision, Doctor?* The idea that anything would be acceptable to take in place of my sight was ridiculous.

As the years have passed, though, I see that letter in a much different light. It has become apparent to me that, as my physical vision has declined, it seems that there is some kind of internal vision that has been increasing. Things I could never see, I seem to know. It is not great psychic ability, don't get me wrong. I believe that it is a "benefit" that the Holy Spirit has afforded me.

This benefit has been an important part of my work as a mental health counselor. There is no doubt in my mind that my work is because of my vision loss, not in spite of it.

It is not always easy for a person to share openly all that should be shared when they are telling me about their situations. Yet, there have been many times when I will hear a question or a response coming out of my mouth that seems to have diverted around my own thinking path. It is often something that is necessary for a client to share the root of the issue they need to share.

That process has amazed me, but I can't help but believe that the doctor was right. I have been given "benefits" that I would never have received if God had not provided them. They have made me aware that things I know I would not be able to do successfully are accomplished in spite of my inabilities. God does amazing things!

Even the fact that I am a mental health counselor, at all, is a bit of a miracle. It began even before I finished my Bachelor's Degree in social work I knew that I wanted to do counseling. I knew that I was going to have a Master's Degree someday, but at the time there seemed no way. The only programs I could attend were an hour away from my home and because I was unable to drive, it seemed an impossible situation.

I worked as a Social Worker, but the nagging sense that I needed to enroll in the counseling program at South Dakota State University changed from a "someday" to a "now." I sat at my kitchen counter and called the Admissions office. There were classes being offered right in Sioux Falls, where I lived! I could do the first required classes and then transfer to the campus later. I signed up!

My husband was not excited. I had found funding, but there were always extra costs with going to school.

"How do you plan to get back and forth to the University, once you're done with the classes in town?" he asked. "I can't take you back and forth. I have this job you know."

I understood his attitude. He had been doing double-duty driving for twenty years already—chauffeuring me around town for various reasons, taking our daughters and son to their activities and car-pooling. The last thing he needed was a 2-hour round trip once or twice every week.

"I don't know how I'll get there. I just know that I know that I am supposed to do this NOW!"

I attended my first class at the Sioux Falls satellite. The class was large and I knew no one. We talked about being admitted into the program and the realities of completing the coursework. It was a scary prospect, but I felt energized by it all.

Then, at the second class, I sat across the table from a woman I had never met before. She had big round glasses and very long, naturally curly hair. She chatted easily with everyone.

"Do you plan to go through the whole program?" she asked me a few minutes into the conversation. After I nodded, she said, "Well, I would guess that you are going to need a ride up to Brookings when our classes in Sioux Falls are done, right? Why don't we sign up for classes together? That way, you can always have a ride and I can have someone to ride with me. What do you think?"

Talk about a miracle. I had never imagined how thoroughly planned this adventure would be, but God had clearly made a way where there had been no way that I could see.

Three years later, Allison and I both graduated. She had made a commitment to transport me to all those classes, and she kept her word.

Counseling was such a great fit for me. I was given a position at Lutheran Social Services, where I had done my internship. Leaving long-term care behind, I set forth on my final career.

I had to quit my work as a nurse. I had to quit the Social Work position about the time I was ready to graduate from the counseling program. The amount of paper work and my declining vision combined to make my staying in that role impossible.

Now here I was, at last. I sat back in my chair about a year after coming to work at LSS, and I prayed to God a prayer of thanksgiving for bringing me such a wonderful and fulfilling place to work. *I can do this for the rest of my life!* I thought.

No sooner had that thought entered my mind than I felt the Spirit speaking to me, "Don't get too comfortable here. This is only preparation for what you are going to do."

I was stunned. What more could I do?

Several years went by and nothing happened. Then there was an interesting workshop being offered at the local seminary that I knew I should attend. It was about working with couples, and the Lord knew I needed all the help I could get!

The workshop was great. I learned many things. And, as an added bonus, one of my best friends just "happened" to walk up to the door at the same time I did.

We spent the day together, talking and sharing in between sessions. At lunchtime we stood in line, waiting our turn to walk through the buffet line.

Suddenly, I sensed a very strong message. *This is where you belong.* I wasn't sure what to make of it. I told my friend what I had just experienced. I felt a shiver up my spine.

Surely, I thought, *this must be low blood sugar. I know they have a counseling program here, but I already have a Master's Degree.*

I decided not to make any moves on this strange message unless I had another message. If this were really from God, he would need to speak more clearly to me than that—a neon sign, perhaps?

A year went by. Nothing was happening, but I continued to feel that I was only at LSS temporarily. It was a frustrating time, but I tried to remember that Moses waited forty years before he was shown what to do to help lead his people.

Months later, Mary, a friend of mine, asked me to work with her on a workshop about "Inclusive Worship" for people with various disabling conditions. I agreed.

After presenting at the conference, Mary invited me along to co-present at the conference in Rapid City. The five-hour trip offered an opportunity for lengthy conversation. We talked about purpose and directions we were moving in our lives. Mary had taken a few classes at North American Baptist Seminary, thinking that her work in Inclusive Worship would have more credibility if she had a credential behind her name.

She turned to me. "Rita! You should go to seminary! You would be a perfect Chaplain—with your experience as a nurse and social work and counseling. You would be great!"

OK. Here it is again. Mary doesn't know about my message from the lunch line, I thought to myself.

"Did I ever tell you that I have thought of going to seminary?" I inquired.

"No! Oh, it would be great! You could ride to classes with me!" she offered enthusiastically.

"Mary, even though I would love to be taking classes at seminary, there is no way I could do that. My vision has deteriorated to the point that I can't read books anymore. Even with the magnifying machine I use at work, it would take too long and be too stressful to do it—especially with the amount of reading that seminary education takes."

"Oh, that's too bad," Mary consoled me. "Well, maybe God will make a way. You could have readers, couldn't you?"

I thanked her for the suggestion, but it wasn't a practical plan. If God wanted me to go to seminary, it would take some kind of miracle.

Within a few weeks, wheels started turning. Although it seemed intrusive in my life at the time, a Case Worker at Services to the Blind and Visually Impaired, the agency that had assisted me many ways in the past, wanted to review my file. He said it was standard operating procedure.

Even though I generally did well with acceptance of my diminished sight, this retriggered all kinds of negative feelings in me. Why is this important? Don't they understand the prognosis for RP? Don't they realize how stressful those eye tests are for me?

I felt so angry, my husband tried to calm me down. "Just do what they ask, Rita. They need to do this, so just do the eye test."

It was as awful, or worse, than I had imagined. I had a "Visual Field" examination. It is hard to describe, but let it suffice to say that I wasn't able to find the little flashes of light they asked me to acknowledge. I sat and stared at the black screen, waiting for the flashes, but there were none.

The doctor sat in impersonal detachment as he looked in my eyes and told me of the small residual sight I still had.

"Well, at least I have been able to work," I offered.

"I don't know how you can. You really don't have much vision left at all. And, at this point, there is no hope for a cure."

"There is no hope, short of a miracle!" I replied.

"No, you aren't going to have any miracle. The only miracle that might be available is from the research being done, and frankly, they don't have much to offer. They make it sound like an answer is right around the corner, but you had better plan that it won't be in *your* lifetime."

His words stung like fire. Was he trying to be brutal? He certainly had no empathy training.

The man left the room with me sitting alone in the room. Even though he had just told me I couldn't see anything, he had left me to find my own way out of an unfamiliar place! I stood up and made my way to the door and yelled after him.

"Could you come and help me out of here, please?"

It is hard to imagine that such a negative experience had such a positive result. Even though his report went back to the Case Worker revealing a grossly deteriorated ability to see, the Case Worker, Alan, had a vested interest in helping me. He recognized what I had been trying to deny. If I didn't receive more training and specialized technologies to help me, I wouldn't be able to continue working as a counselor, or anything else.

He prepared a plan, sent me for an assessment at the Rehabilitation Center, and within a few months, he had provided me with the latest technology. This equipment–a computer with a screen reading program, a book scanning program and scanner, a magnifier that attached to the computer screen, and a Braille-equipped "lap-top" device that could interface with my computer–all to make it possible to do things I had lost the ability to do the old way. All this was provided without any cost to me–one set at home and one set at work.

Who could have imagined what that notice of a review months earlier was intended to provide for me.

I prayed for forgiveness from God after that. He had choreographed all those things to provide me equipment I could never have afforded.

Then, it came to me! Seminary was no longer an impossibility! It would be very hard–but not impossible!

I spoke with Karl about the nudging I had been given about attending seminary. He wasn't impressed.

"How would we pay for that? Is there any funding?" He wanted to know.

"No, There isn't much for funding. I would need to borrow the money. But, I just have a feeling that, if God wants me to go to seminary, he will make it possible. I don't think we will have to pay for it, somehow."

If the money had shown up in the mailbox one day, I wouldn't have been surprised. It didn't. There was no money. Maybe I was wrong. Maybe this was just an attempt on my part to cope with losing my eyesight–I didn't know.

The time of agonizing over God's call to me went on day and night. I sought the Lord's answer to me, but I never received it.

In June, it seemed that it would be necessary to talk with someone about the practical realities of attending seminary. I met with Melissa. There were no scholarships or grants available–they had all been given out already for the next fall. If I wanted to, I could fill out paperwork and see if there was anything that I could qualify for in Federal loans and grants.

I completed it all. Maybe there was still hope.

I decided, after praying, that I needed to have something to affirm my call to seminary. So far, things weren't falling into place the way I thought they would. If I didn't receive any funding, I would take that to mean that I was not intended to attend seminary–at least, not now.

The phone rang. I heard Melissa's voice on the other end.

"Rita, I have news for you. One of the scholarships that had been awarded for fall has been returned. The person who received it was unable to attend this fall. It will pay for your books every semester of your three years. Do you want it?"

Of course, I wanted it! It was not only a large amount of money off my yearly costs, it was the sign I desperately needed to let me know that God was taking me to the seminary.

Even though I felt I *had* to go, I continued to doubt my call. It seemed the others in my classes were so certain of what the Lord had called them to do. I only knew what I did *not* feel called to do.

I knew I was to enroll in the Master of Divinity program, but I wasn't supposed to be a pastor. I knew I was to preach. I knew I needed to use the music God had given me. I knew I was to reach out to people who felt disenfranchised from the traditional church. All those who would never be found in a church pew on Sundays still needed God. How I was to do it or where, I had no clue.

I didn't know the answers. I had to trust that God would keep me informed on a "need to know" basis.

I began classes in the fall. One of the professors asked that we write a short story about how we were called to ministry. An event came back to me that I had tucked way in the back of my mind.

I remembered when we had a visit at our church by a missionary and his family. They were serving in the country known then as Tanganyika, Africa. I looked in amazement at the Python skin and elephant tail they brought to show us. There was something that fascinated me even more. They told us about children who had never heard of Jesus before.

I left there thinking hard about what they said. I walked off alone, feeling the dew on the grass against my bare feet, breathing in the air of that summer night and talking with my friend.

"Jesus, I would love to go and tell others about you. If you want me to go to the mission field, I will. I will go anywhere you want– Africa, or China, or any place you need me to go. I just don't want to be one of those missionaries that stays in their own neighborhood and tells people about the gospel in their own town. Not because I am not wanting them to hear, but I just feel too shy to do that. I'll go anyplace else, though."

It took a long time from that night to my surrender to his call. I had put limits on what I would do. I wanted to keep just a little part that I said "No" to. So, of course, that was the part God still wanted. He didn't need someone who would not be fully surrendered.

I was young. I never told anyone about that call until I was in my 40's. I thought everyone felt called like that. And, it seems that the scripture tells us that we are each called to have a part in building up the body of Christ (Eph. 4: 1-16).

I told my supervisor in my counseling program about that call. I mentioned that I was sure we all felt called like that, to do Christ's work in some way.

"No," he said. "I never had that kind of call. I think you experienced something different than most of us."

Another woman sitting in the room agreed. They told me they had never had such an experience.

It seems sad to me that I didn't follow up on that call for so long. Yet, I have to trust that God moves us in his own timing, not ours.

It was clear as I looked past over my life that I never had a time when I didn't feel that God would call me someday to his full-time work. It was my expectation that it would come in a clearer way. It never was an audible voice or another person coming up and saying, "You should be in ministry, Rita."

It was always there in my gut. God had a plan for me. He had a plan for me. He had a plan for me.

Some place, I don't know where or when it was, a minister talked about being completely willing to follow God's call. He talked about signing up for what was ahead without knowing what it was. He suggested that we take a piece of paper and sign it on the bottom of the page, "I will" and sign our name. God could then fill out the top part of that paper with whatever he wanted to put.

I did that. I went home and prayerfully wrote" I will" on the page and signed my name. I had forgotten about that until just as I write this now. I came to a place of willingness long before God called me to attend seminary.

Do you suppose God didn't use me until I was attending classes at North American Baptist Seminary? I don't think so. It seems that he worked through me throughout my life. All I had to do was to be willing to be used.

The only thing that was clear as I attended classes was that I loved the things I was learning. I ate it up! Whatever was in the future, God alone knew. All that I was required to do was to walk in obedience to him.

For There Is One Lord

Words and music by Rita Weber
Copyright © 2002 by Rita Weber

Lead a life that is worthy of the call to which you're called
In humility and gentleness, with patience
In love, bear with each other.
Keep the Spirit's unity, making every effort in the bonds of peace.

Refrain
For there is one Lord
And there is one faith.
There is one baptism, one hope of our call.
There is one body, There is one Spirit.
For there is one God and Father of us all.

All the gifts Christ has given for the work of ministry
Will equip us each to grow and build Christ's body.
'til all parts are knit together in the unity of faith
Grow in knowledge, in Christ's likeness, and in love.

To Refrain

For there is one God and Father, who is above all and through all.
One God and Father of us all.

Changing Landscapes

Seminary was the most challenging experience I have ever gone through. My husband was not supportive—he couldn't understand why I was creating thousands of dollars worth of debt and looking to launch a ministry when he was ready to think about retiring. He couldn't help but feel betrayed by what he viewed as rejection of his faith, which did not support women in ministry.

We had never had many conflicts in our marriage before. This put our marriage vows to the test—not on my part, but on his. And, I couldn't blame him for feeling as he did. He couldn't be expected to understand this when I really didn't understand it, myself.

There wasn't much I could do. I prayed for him and for me.

My first day at seminary, at the orientation luncheon, the Lord hooked me up with a woman who had also been working in a career as a counselor. We connected so easily—she was clearly a woman deeply committed to her walk with Christ. In response to the horrific attack on 9/11/01, we began to meet together to pray for the world and the threat of terror, as well as for the terrorists themselves, that God would change their hearts.

Our prayer connection lasted throughout our time at seminary. We met every week and began to expand our prayer concerns to things that were personally challenging, too. Our prayers covered many things—including my husband, Karl.

At the beginning of 2003, I was beginning to see a softening in Karl's heart toward my work at seminary. It wasn't dramatic, but by the time I finished my studies in December of 2003, Karl's changed attitude had become visible to other students. He picked me up and dropped me off and carried around my reading machine without complaint. We began praying together every morning for concerns for the day.

My mother had a sign she used to keep posted in the grocery store she ran. The sign read, "Prayer Changes Things."

It was true. I didn't have any way to change Karl's opinion of my attendance at seminary. I wasn't even sure how to pray for him. I just prayed and asked God to help him.

It seems that we often overlook the most powerful tool at our disposal—prayer. We may not know how to pray effectively.

In Romans 8:26, Paul writes that, "even though we don't know how to pray as we ought, the Spirit prays on our behalf with groanings and utterings."

One day several years ago, my son came home for a visit from the small community where he had recently started working as a policeman. He had been home for only a short while when he looked at me with an accusing look and asked, "Mom, have you been praying for me?"

"Of course, Chris. I always pray for you."

"No, I mean, have you been praying that I will stay safe?"

"Yes, Chris. I always pray that you will be safe."

"I thought so!" He responded. "Every time there is a robbery or some kind of action, I'm either off for the day or on another shift. Please don't quit praying that I will be safe, but could you change it so I could still have things happen?"

In Hebrews we are told to "come boldly before the throne of grace." God wants to do things for us. He is eager to help us, but he will not intrude on our lives. He always waits to be invited, before he steps into our circumstances.

If Only You Will Pray

Words and music by Rita Weber
Copyright © 2003 by Rita Weber

What is it that you need?
What will you ask the Lord today
As you come boldly before his throne of grace?
What could he do for you, if only you would ask him to?
He's waiting, now, to answer you, if only you would pray.

Do you need a heart of thanksgiving
To see all that God has done?
Or a place to lay the burdens that you carry?
When you take delight in the presence
Of this Precious, Holy One,
He will give you the desires of your heart.

What is it that you need?
What will you ask the Lord today?
As you come boldly before his throne of grace?
What could he do for you, if only you would ask him to?
He's waiting, now, to answer you, if only you would pray.

Do you need to ask for forgiveness
For some sinful things you've done?
Or to let go of things you hold against another?
Do you need to ask for a healing of your body, mind, or soul?
He can do far more than you could think to ask.

What is it that you need?
What will you ask the Lord today?
As you come boldly before his throne of grace?
What could he do for you, if only you would ask him to?
He's waiting, now, to answer you, if only you would pray.

Sweet Dream *Chapter 9*

During the summer before I began my seminary classes, I went to a lake in northern Minnesota for an annual family gathering. The day was hot—over 100 degrees. My sisters and I headed into town for our lunch, as was our usual custom. After light lunch and heavy conversation, we headed back to the cabin. Normally, we would have done a little antiquing. Today, it was just too hot.

When we arrived back at the lake, I was suddenly very tired. I slipped off into the room designated for Karl and me. There, I stretched out on my back. I had never taken a nap at the lake before. Today, I had no choice.

Immediately, I fell into a deep, deep, sleep. That was unusual for me. I am just not a person who falls asleep quickly. I don't have any idea how long I had been asleep, but a violent shaking awakened me. At first I thought someone was shaking the bed or maybe it was an earthquake. I had never felt one, but that was what I imagined it would feel like. Then I realized that it wasn't anyone shaking the bed. The violent shaking was from within me!

The only way I can describe this to you is to liken it to movies when astronauts in training are breaking free of the gravitational pull of the earth. This violent shaking stopped and suddenly I, the essence of who I am, broke free from the earthly realm and began to move very fast through time and space. I saw nothing. I felt nothing. I only knew that I was propelling through a great distance.

When I came to a place of stillness, I experienced a sensation I have never known before or since. I knew that I was in the presence of God. I knew that I had died and that my soul was free from its earthly body. I could feel the love of God. It poured over me and around me and *through* me. I had never felt so totally and sublimely joyous and content in all my life. There was no fear or worry. There was only this incredible love saturating me.

I began praising God with all my being, praising and thanking him for his wonderful love, praising and thanking him that all I had believed throughout my life had been true. He was even more wonderful and loving than my mind had thought possible.

I had always wondered how it would be in heaven one day—thanking and praising God all the time. I am a person who likes variety. Now, I could think of nothing I would choose to do other than stay in this ecstasy, praising God and loving him in response to this wonderful love I felt.

A thought entered my consciousness. What about my family? There down on the earth was my husband and my children, and all my extended family. They would feel sad when they came into the bedroom and saw that I had died.

No sooner had this thought been formed than I realized that this wonderful love that God was showing to me was the same love he had for each of them. God would take care of them and I could just enjoy being in his presence.

Boom! My being came back into the lifeless body on the bed once again. I lay there crying out to God, "No! Please, God don't make me come back! Please let me stay with you!"

It was awful; I could feel the weight of this earthly body and the pull of gravity on it. I lay there, uncertain of how much time had passed. The only thing I was certain of was that I had gone from this world into the spiritual realm. I had been allowed to know a taste of how glorious that will be one day when I am in the presence of God Almighty.

I was sad. I wanted to go back. Later, I lay in the lake on my back and looked up at the sky. "Please, Lord. Please let me be with you."

Obviously, the Lord has a different plan for me. I need to fulfill the work that has been prepared for me to do and then—then…

You may think, *she was only dreaming. She didn't really die.*

Clearly, I don't have any way to prove anything. All I know for certain is that I no longer fear death. I don't know how long God intends for me to remain here, but when he calls me home, I will be ready.

I have changed how I see those who are called by death to be in their heavenly home. No matter how young, they are the fortunate and blessed among us. This world can never compare with what lies in store for us in God's presence.

There Will Come A Time

Words and music by Rita Weber
Copyright © 2003 by Rita Weber

There will come a time
When there will be no parting,
When our broken hearts will be made whole
By the One who loves us best.
But, until that day,
We must face tomorrow,
Living with the sorrow
And missing those who've gone away.
If only we could see the face and hear the laughter of those
    who've gone before—
Free from earthly strain, free from all the pain
Free to live once more.

There will come a time when we will be together,
Sharing life forever in the presence of Almighty God.
For, when we meet Christ face-to-face and
See his glory
Our tears will all be dried.
There in heaven's home, loved ones we have known
Will welcome us inside.

There will come a time when there will be no parting.

Plan "A" *Chapter 10*

Seminary is done. The Master of Divinity diploma is sitting in its leather binder. I still work two days a week as a counselor and do "pulpit supply," filling in for pastors who need to be away for a Sunday. I share the music that has been given to me whenever the opportunity presents itself.

Is there more to God's plan for me? I don't know.

Several years ago, I was peeling wallpaper off my bathroom wall. I love jobs like that. They don't require any mental effort, so it is a free pass to spend a day in reflection and prayer. I have done some of my best thinking while peeling wallpaper!

On this particular day, I was busy thinking about how God always has a plan. When I couldn't be a nurse anymore, he opened the door to do Social Work. When the paperwork became too much for me there, he allowed me to do counseling.

I prayed, *Thank you, God, that you always have a Plan B!*

Out of nowhere, my thoughts were challenged.

"No! You are wrong! There is no Plan B. Your vision loss was a surprise to you—not to me. You are still on Plan A!

What a glorious thought. How can one help but praise a God who operates like that! He knows everything that we will face long before we do. His plan includes every thing that we see as a negative. That is what the verse in Romans 8:28 means when it says he makes all things work for good. The bigger the negative is, the greater the potential for it being a positive when God is in the picture.

Please don't be confused. I am not a "Pollyanna" about my disability. I go through a lot of stuff because of not being able to see. It isn't easy not to be able to have the independence of driving a car. Life would have been just fine if I could have been able to continue working as a nurse. We would have had a much easier time of things financially, I think. It is hard to have to depend on others to pick out clothes when I go shopping. Everyone means well, but each one only looks at things they personally think are attractive. They may not show me something that I would love to wear.

My daughter said to me one day, "Mom, I wonder what your taste in clothes is like. You always end up dressing in clothes like the person who took you shopping wears!

Those aren't the worst things in the world. I have more to be grateful for than I have to complain about.

It is important for people who are not disabled themselves to understand something about living with a chronic condition like mine, though. This is not to gain your sympathy. That would not be useful. I only share it so you can understand how you can be helpful to others. Or, if you struggle with your own chronic disability, you may feel free to see how my experience compares with your own.

First, the losses associated with having a disability like mine are multiple. They affect so many parts of daily life that I don't choose to enumerate them here. Just know that the grieving over those losses is never done. I have good days, and I have not-so-good days. I don't need you to fix anything—you can't. Just understand that I have to work hard to pull myself up and keep moving sometimes.

Just because I have been blind for many years, doesn't mean that I am done grieving it. Just when I feel pretty good about things, I can have something happen to remind me of how much I wish I could see. That is a normal thing in dealing with a chronic loss. It is not useful for me when others think I am in denial or try to analyze my response to blindness.

I need to be included in life. If you think I can't do a particular activity, don't pass me by. If I can't do it, I'll tell you. It feels much better to be asked and have the option of saying I can't do that, than to be excluded. And, I might have a way of doing a thing that you would never guess. Just ask!

It is important that I feel capable and useful. If there are things to be done in the kitchen, for instance, don't assume it would be too difficult and tell me to go in the other room and sit with the kids. Find something that I *can* do. If you don't know what that is, ask. If I don't feel up to it, I can tell you that.

When you meet someone with a disability, do not assume that they do not work or have a life. Ask questions just like you would ask to anyone. You may be surprised at what you discover.

Try to understand that many things in this world are sources of suffering. God does allow suffering—look at Paul if you don't believe it. Even when Paul asked God to remove the "thorn" three times, God chose not to do it.

Part of my healing in the past was only possible after I studied that passage. I had been struggling to understand the reason that God, though many others and I had prayed, never gave me a healing.

I was raised believing strongly that God has the power to heal. When I was a young girl, my Dad took me to church where a faith healer was holding special services. Though Dad didn't have any knowledge of my genetic disease, he sought prayer to heal a weak muscle in my eye that caused one of my eyes to drift off to the side.

"Now, Rita, you know that God can heal you, right?"

"Yes."

"Good. Because, you have to *really* believe it or it won't happen. You have to have faith. Do you have faith?"

Dad's heart was in the right place, but my eyes weren't healed. Of course that meant that I didn't have enough faith. That was how I interpreted that. And, for many years, I continued to struggle over the fact that my faith wasn't strong enough for God to help me.

After I was diagnosed with the RP, I prayed more than ever. But, no matter how much I prayed and believed, my miracle never came. I began to consider the other possibilities. Maybe it was because I had committed too many sins, and God was punishing me. Or, maybe God just didn't love me as much as other people.

It was only after I read about Paul that I was able to get perspective on the matter. There was no one in the New Testament who was more of an apostle than Paul. Yet, he hadn't been given the healing of the "thorn" he suffered with either.

Paul said that he was told by God, "My grace is sufficient for you. My strength is made perfect in your weakness." (II Corinthians 12:9).

Suffering has a purpose. God can use it for many reasons. Do not assume when things cause suffering in people's lives that it is because of sinfulness. A quick read of John 9 will reveal that Jesus tried to teach his disciples that the standard notion that a physical ailment must be because someone sinned was wrong! In the story shared, the man was born blind so God's glory could be revealed.

Jesus not only had compassion on the "man born blind," he shared a very special revelation with him. In the days when Jesus was on the earth, people who had a physical deformity or disease or blindness were not allowed to come into the temple. This man, blind from birth was free now that Jesus had healed him to go in and worship God like other people did. The Pharisees and Chief Priests threw him out of the temple for claiming that Jesus had healed him. Jesus had compassion on him again, and when he found the man, he revealed to him that he was God. The man's spiritual blindness healed, he bowed down and worshipped Jesus.

Jesus didn't simply tolerate people with special needs. He had compassion on them—he suffered *with* them. He welcomed them into his presence.

Things haven't changed that much in 2,000 years. Many of our churches are no more willing to welcome people with disabilities than the Priests in the Temple had been. When the Americans With Disabilities Act became the law of the land, many ramps popped up at the entrances of church buildings. Unfortunately, welcoming people with special needs goes way beyond putting in a ramp. Our hearts must have a genuine welcoming to all individuals. Each person is a creation of God. Each one is his beloved. Each one needs to know how much He loves and cares for him/her.

It seems to me, because of my own disability, I need to know God even more than able-bodied people need him. There are so many messages in this world that declare me to be "less than." It is only in God that I have found my true identity. It is only in God that I can be greater than—greater than the obstacles, greater than disappointments, greater than my own ability.

Jesus wanted all people to be able to worship him. He had healing for the man's blindness, physical and spiritual. Those who thought they had perfect vision were left truly blind.

That's enough of that. You get the idea. To sum up, ask, include, listen, and don't assume anything!

When we were studying Social Ministry of the Church in seminary, I did reading about the people in our society who are invisible. If you are not an invisible person, yourself, you will need to take my word for this. There are people who cannot see people like me.

I remember one night when I attended a women's prayer group with a friend of mine. After the program was finished, I went over to try to connect with others who had attended that night, while my friend took care of her responsibilities for clean up.

I went up to a woman I had met before. She was in a conversation, but I spoke her name and tried to get her attention several times. She could not see me at all. I decided she was in an important discussion so I moved on. Each group of women I approached scattered like I had the plague and not one of them spoke a word to me.

I gave up. I sat down on a chair by the door and waited to leave. Just before my friend came, a wonderful woman sat down with me. She only made a bit of small talk, but it was such a gift to me!

That's Who I Am

Words and music by Rita Weber
Copyright © 2003 by Rita Weber

Who am I?
You see a broken human being with no value and no worth.
Who am I?
Rejected and forsaken by all of those who question
Why I was ever given birth.
But, I have something to tell you now, before you turn away.
If you will listen, this is what I have to say,

I am a beautiful creation of the great, eternal God,
Created in his image for his purpose.
I am a sinner who's forgiven,
Washed clean by the Blood of the Lamb.
I'm a child of the King of Kings, That's who I am!

Who am I?
Invisible to all of those who see with earthly eyes.
Who am I?
Unheard by deafened ears of those
Who choose not to listen to the sound of human cries.
But, I have something to say about my true identity.
It is the one that Jesus Christ the Lord has given me.

I am a beautiful creation of the great, eternal God,
Created in his image for his purpose.
I am a sinner who's forgiven,
Washed clean by the Blood of the Lamb.
I'm a child of the King of Kings. That's who I am!

Parting The Waters

When others see me with a white cane, they make assumptions. It may seem that I have always carried one and that it is a natural part of who I am.

In reality, the cane is pretty new to me. It has become a tool I depend on now, but seventeen years ago, when I first admitted my need for it, admitting was a very hard thing to do.

A case manager had given me a cane to have in case I needed it in the late '70's. I kept it tucked deep inside a drawer. I didn't need it, and I did not want people to think I did!

As my vision declined, I was becoming more and more isolated inside my home. It was not safe to travel anywhere that was unfamiliar. I had tripped and had close calls crossing the street enough times to be a little scared. I couldn't use that cane, though. What if people thought I couldn't see!

In the late '80's, Paul Pirtle, my caseworker, convinced me that it was time to do training at the rehabilitation center in town. I had been dragging my feet on that for several years. Now I was becoming aware of my declining ability to do my housework and other normal functions. I knew he was right. I needed to have help in finding new ways to do the activities of daily life.

Help came in the form of a homemaker who helped me with a few hints and gadgets for cooking and sewing. There were crafts that could be done with no sight at all. There were opportunities to go out into the community and learn assertiveness skills in restaurants. It all was useful. I didn't feel so helpless as I faced my future.

An older gentleman appeared at the center one day. "Hi, Rita. I'm going to be your mobility instructor."

I shook his hand and shook deep inside, too. "I really don't know if I need a white cane," I explained to him gently.

"Well, let's just go out and I'll teach you a few things. Then, if you get to a place where you think you need it, you're ready."

Ray was an older man who was called out of retirement to help me. We went out to different residential areas where he would make me put on a blindfold, and then we would walk. It was hard to keep my bearings. There was always a need to mentally think about the direction I was going and how many turns I had made. That was very challenging, especially since we talked as we walked.

It was surprising, what I found out about being blind during those lessons. Did you know that wind for a blind person is like fog to a sighted one? When the wind was blowing, not only was it cold, it was hard to get clues about my surroundings.

He helped me to pay attention to the changes in sound as I walked down the street, the deadness that was evident when there was a vehicle parked in a driveway or a structure close to the sidewalk.

Those were cold winter days. We walked as much as we could, then we would find someplace warm to talk. That was definitely the best part. Ray would tell me about his days in the service or working at the School for the Blind. We joked and laughed and forgot about the stressful lessons.

We had been walking around in different locations for several weeks when he turned to me in the cab of the van and said in a serious tone, "Rita, it's time that you get out in the public and use that cane of yours."

My stomach turned. "I don't think I can, Ray."

"Why not?"

"I don't think I'm ready."

"You know, Rita. You have been walking around not seeing for a long time. People who are around you often already know you can't see. You haven't been fooling anybody. You were just fooling yourself. I know this is hard to do for the first time," he said with a gentleness in his voice, "but you need to think of someplace where you can use it where you will be the most comfortable. You think about that tonight and tomorrow you can tell me where you are going to make your debut."

I knew someplace in my heart that Ray was right. It was so hard to think how embarrassing it would feel, actually walking out in front of people I knew. *Oh, God, please help me do this, I prayed that night.*

It didn't take long to figure out where I would do my truth walk. The choir was meeting that night, as it did every Thursday night. Tonight, I would walk in there with my cane, I determined.

Ray and I had our lesson that morning. When he asked I told him my plan.

"Good. You will do just fine. You know, most people will be just fine with this, and if there is anyone who isn't, what do they matter anyway?"

My husband drove me up to the front of the church and I stood out on the sidewalk, taking a few deep breaths before I went inside. I had gone into that building and into the sanctuary many times. Surely, I could do it now.

As I walked into the darkened foyer without Karl to guide me, I realized how dependent I had become on him. I had to run my forearm against the wall where the doors were until I found the handle. Then, taking one last breath for courage and breathing a little prayer, I walked in.

The choir was up in front practicing. Slowly, I began my long journey to the front. I was nearly half way to my destination when something remarkable happened. I heard someone clapping. One by one the choir members stopped singing and began applauding. What a gift that was to me.

All my fears and embarrassment faded as I heard shouts of, "Way to go, Rita! Yeah, Rita!"

Ray was a wise man. He helped me to overcome a great obstacle I never could have surmounted without him.

What I discovered after that night was that this little white stick offered more help than I had ever imagined. When I was in a public place, I never had to explain that I needed help because I was visually impaired. Help was offered to me automatically. If I walked through a crowded mall, the people in front of me scattered. Ray had told me it would be like a bunch of chickens running to get out of my way, or like Moses parting the waters of the Red Sea!

My cane has become a very important part of life to me. I rarely am without it. Even in my dreams, I am usually carrying my cane.

One important lesson I have learned is that when I am walking and I pay attention to what it is telling me, by sound or feel, I can be safe in my journey. If things around me distract me, or if I begin to think for one minute that I don't need it, I get into trouble.

Isn't that like you and I in our walk with Christ? As long as we pay attention to his leading and focus on what he is telling us, things go smoothly. It is when we are distracted by other things or become confident in our own ability that we fall off the path.

Second Corinthians 5:7 says, "For we walk by faith, not by sight." In other words, this walk is so easy we can do it with our eyes closed? Well, maybe we rely on our faith in Christ, not on what our earthly eyes tell us.

Several years ago, between the time I graduated with my Social Work degree and my time at the rehab center, I worked for a couple years for a professional organization. I had an office in my house, which worked well with my elementary-aged children.

The salary wasn't great, but I had a long title, and I was given a chance to travel to the national headquarters in Washington D.C. for a few meetings.

The first trip out there, I went alone. Karl was staying home with the kids. I could tell he was afraid to send me off on my own to a big city I had never been in before.

I assured him about my travel arrangements. "I will get off the plane, get on a shuttle to go to the subway, and then it is only a couple blocks to the hotel. I will be just fine."

I wasn't as confident in my ability to do this as I let on, but I didn't want him to worry. I had no white cane with me then. I would need to ask for help, that was my only option.

The flight went fine. When I entered the luggage area and picked up my bag, I noticed a sign overhead that pointed to the shuttle, just as I had been told.

I had never even seen a subway. There wasn't much light in the area where the tickets had to be purchased. I stood in front of the machine, uncertain where I was going and unsure of how to use the machine to pay my fare even if I had known.

I was praying hard when I was approached by a couple dressed like hippies from the '60s. I thought they must be angels, because they asked if I needed help. When I admitted I did, they helped me buy the ticket, rode with me on the subway, and before they left the train, they told me, "The next stop will be where you get off. You need to use your ticket in the turnstile to get out of the subway, so don't lose it!"

I was on my own again. My ticket was so damp from my sweaty palms; it took several tries to make it open the turnstile. The guard looked at me with suspicion and made an accusation that I was trying to ride farther than I had paid to ride. I told him I hadn't—just as the ticket clicked open the gate.

I asked him how to get to my hotel, noticing that I had a half hour to arrive there before my meeting. It was cutting it close, but it was only a couple blocks.

I left the subway station and started walking to cross the busy street. I made it safely to the meridian. Then I stopped to readjust my suitcase.

The coat I was wearing had been comfortable in South Dakota that morning, but now, the sun was beating down. I took the coat off, flung it over my arm, picked up the suitcase and started crossing when the light turned for me.

A car turned the corner so close to me that I felt it against my coat! Didn't drivers know about pedestrian right-of-way out here?

I walked down the street in the direction the guard had pointed out. I walked and walked and walked, but there was still no hotel in sight.

It was nearly a mile before I spotted the sign for the hotel in the distance. I picked up my pace a bit. That half hour was used up, and I still had a few blocks to go.

At last I arrived at my destination. I walked in, readjusted my things and began to walk with renewed confidence across the lobby to the front desk twenty feet in front of me.

What happened next was disastrous! I had no depth perception. The three steps down to the lower desk area came as a total surprise. I felt myself falling, bumping against the hard steps and landing in a heap on the lobby floor. My pantyhose were shredded and so was my spirit. I sat there and began to cry. I could have put up with any one of my misfortunes of the last hour, but this last one was more than I could bear.

Hotel personnel ran from every corner, certain of a lawsuit. They were kind and helped me to a chair where I could weep in private.

"You just sit here and take it easy. Are you all right? Do you think anything is broken?"

A supervisor type appeared. "We want our paramedic to have a look and make sure you're all right, Ma'am."

The paramedic bent down and began to examine the knee that had taken the brunt of the fall. A woman from behind the front desk came rushing over with a telephone.

"Mrs. Weber? Are you Mrs. Weber?"

"Why, yes. I am," I answered.

"It's your husband," she explained.

Oh, no. I had promised I would call Karl as soon as I arrived. I didn't plan on arriving so late. I knew he would be concerned.

"What's going on?" Karl demanded as I picked up the phone. "I called a while ago and they said you weren't there yet. I called again and the woman said, 'she can't speak to you right now. She's with the paramedic!'"

Of all the things my husband did not need to hear, his greatest worry had seemed to be happening. After all, he had warned me not to take a subway from the airport.

I hurried to calm his worst fear, received a clean bill of health, changed panty hose, and resumed my schedule without incident. But, that was the last time I ever traveled anywhere alone! I know the Lord is with me and I can trust him to help me, no matter where I go, but my husband wants to be with me, too!

I Am There

Words and music by Rita Weber
Copyright © 2004 by Rita Weber

Stranded on my journey, wishing I was home,
Feeling so abandoned and alone.
Crying out to Jesus, "Oh, Lord, what should I do?
I need a little help to get me through."
The two looked more like hippies than like angels standing there.
They came to me that day
To help me on my way.
God was faithful in answering my prayer.

For the Lord said,
"I will never leave you.
I will not forget you,
For your name is written here on the palms of my hands."
"I will never leave you,
I will not forget you.
Just call my name.
I Am there."

"Do you think a mother could
Forget her nursing child?
Yet, I tell you, even if she could,
I will not abandon you,
I'll be right by your side.
I will hear you when you call.
I will catch you if you fall.
You are never alone,
For I Am there."

Destined On Arrival

The sun was glistening on the bumps of the plastic seat covers. I moved my fingers over them, feeling small little particles of glass. Barb's voice was in the background somewhere, though I couldn't see her. She was screaming and crying. Mom's voice came in contrast, soothing, calming. "It's all right, Barb, it's all right. Jesus is here with us right now. It will all be fine."

I faded away again, and then I heard the sound of a male voice that I couldn't recognize. "Come here, honey. Put your arms around my neck. I'm going to take you out and lay you on the ground. OK?"

I felt tired, but I managed to open my eyes just a slit to see one of the most handsome fellows I had ever seen. I didn't know who he was, but I was quite pleased to have my arms around his neck!

There were glimpses of sun, the stubble of the field, and awareness that I was being placed into an ambulance. I lay on the floor of what seemed to be a long station wagon. I could see a red cross on its back window. Occasionally I would open my eyes to see trees passing overhead.

There was a moan next to me. It was Ginny. She was moaning and crying, but I couldn't see her. My best friend of the last couple years lay on a gurney in the ambulance next to me. I wanted to touch her, but I was too weak, so I just talked instead.

"Don't cry, Ginny . You will be all right. Sh-h."

If there was anyone else in the ambulance with us, I was unaware of them. It seemed that it was just Ginny and I. I drifted away again.

My eyes opened just enough to see a glimpse of my surroundings. I heard no sounds, but there were these beings, all in white, that seemed to be floating around the room.

Heaven? Could this be heaven?

I was trying my best to discern clues to my location when a sudden urge overcame me, and I began to relieve myself of my stomach contents. An arm from one of the nurse-nuns guided me to turn, aiming the emesis neatly into a metal basin. It was red, not normal stuff.

Nope. I'm not in heaven! I concluded.

Ginny's injuries were very serious, including a severe concussion and facial lacerations. She was unconscious for a couple days. My own inability to stay awake gave everything a surreal quality. Even when I could hear what was going on around me. I wasn't strong enough to move. I felt much like a woman in a movie I had seen that had been given a drug. She couldn't move, and she was buried alive. Even though she was yelling at the top of her lungs to the people around her, no one could hear anything.

A few of my family members were talking near me. "What's wrong with her?" a voice said.

"She's hemorrhaging from her kidney," the answer came back.

So that was it! I tried hard to move something to let them know I was all right—even a little wiggle of a finger—but I couldn't move. I was too weak. I fell back into the haze again.

Except for a little twitch of my stomach when I heard the word "hemorrhage," I had no fear. I had been at peace all the while.

That Memorial Day in 1966 had been gorgeous in central Minnesota. Dad had announced just that morning that he was taking us to the car races in Howard Lake, and we could invite the Olsen girls to come along.

Ginny and Barb were eager to go with us. They had never been to the car races either.

I dressed in my new white cut-off jeans and a little red plaid shirt. Even I had to admit, I was looking pretty cute! I stuffed the $2.50 I had earned babysitting into my pocket and walked around outside, pacing with the sheer excitement of it all.

Our new Chevy Impala was a big sedan. Mom, Dad, and Susie were in the front seat; Ginny , Lynn, Barb , and I were packed into the back. And we were, literally, "off to the races!"

Our adventure stopped short a mile north of town when a car driven by a young teenager ran the stop sign, plowing into the driver's side of the car. After flipping around, the car came to rest in a field. Mom, Dad, Ginny and I had received the brunt of the impact.

The circumstances must have appeared bleak for those looking on. My mother, also hurt and a fellow patient in the hospital stood by my side. It was the middle of the night.

"What's the matter?" she questioned. "I heard you moaning."

I had not been aware that I was moaning, but now that she asked, I felt the severe pain that was seizing my gut. I realized for the first time that I had been crying in my sleep.

I felt her familiar hand on my forehead stroking back my hair as she had done so many other times. She began to pray softly, "Dear Lord, Jesus. Please come and take this pain from Rita. Please help her to rest."

Whether her prayer and presence lasted longer, I don't know. I fell off into the most blissful sleep, never experiencing that terrible stomach pain again.

Mom's reassurance that Jesus was with us was true. I could feel such peace. If I had died, it would have been all right for me, but I knew that we were going to recover.

A couple weeks later, the doctor came in and sat on the edge of my bed. He looked serious. "Rita, you are about to leave the hospital. But, I want you to know something. When I examined you out in that field after the accident, I didn't think you would be alive by the time we had you at the hospital. You were in very deep shock from the bleeding from your kidney, and there wasn't much we could do for you. Now, here you are doing so much better. It's really a miracle."

The reason that God allowed me to go through that experience is unclear to me, even forty years later. The important thing I learned from it was that God had a reason why my life was spared. It seemed then, and it seems now, that nothing can bring my death unless the Lord allows it. That is a liberating thought. I should have died, but God has given me life. It is his life.

In Him We Live

Words and music by Rita Weber
Copyright © 2003 by Rita Weber

Refrain
In him, we live, and move, and have our being.
Our God who made all the world
Has given life to you and me.
In him, we live, and move, and have our being.
Created in your image, Lord,
Please help us live our destiny.

Our God doesn't live in shrines of human making.
Our undertakings are not done to meet his needs.
For he is the Lord of Heaven.
He made the nations.
To his creation, he gives life
And the breath we breathe.

To Refrain

Like clay on the potter's wheel
Your hands have formed us.
Now, Lord, transform us
By your love's consuming fire.
So we may be vessels fit to share your story,
To bring you glory, to be all that you desire.

To Refrain

Lord, you give us life.
Please make us all you meant for us to be.

Without Warning

The morning was dark and cold. The February snow and wind made the warmth of the bed and the flannel nightgown and two sisters' bodies a cozy place to stay.

Danny's voice broke into my sleeping. He spoke in a loud whisper. "Get up! You have to get up!"

"Oh-h. Leave me alone!" I pulled the covers up over my head.

"No! You have to get up! There's been an accident."

This last bit of news jarred me from my sleepiness. I woke up and tried to make him be truthful–to admit it was just something he said to motivate us to get up.

"It's true," he insisted," still in his loud whisper. "Dad was in an accident this morning."

I slid out of bed, hitting the cold bedroom floor and moving out toward the light of the kitchen. There my mother sat, head in her hands, weeping from the depths of her spirit.

The foggy morning in the darkness of five o'clock had hid the huge train that had stalled across the tracks a few miles from our home in Albright's. Dad and Roy, traveling to their construction jobs, had seen it too late. There was no way to stop on the icy, snow-packed road. Roy slammed on his brakes, but the unmarked train–no flares or warning lights of any kind–loomed before them. The car crumpled into the side of that great iron mountain, throwing Dad through the windshield.

I was only nine at the time, but I knew it was serious. Just Mom's reaction was different than anything I had experienced before. And, she didn't talk to us. My brothers talked to her. It was as if these young teenagers were now the adults, guiding my usually strong and capable mother through the uncharted waters she was crossing.

Lynn, Susie, and I were home. Our neighbor, Ruth came over. She tried to put on a comforting front as she scrubbed the floor and talked with us. Normally, her husband, Eric, would have been in the ride too. Today, a touch of providential flu had prevented that.

At last, she decided that Lynn and I might do better if we were to go to school. We were used to walking the mile to Maple Grove, even in the winter. But today, Ruth gave us a ride in the car.

We went in, an hour late. The teacher said, "A diller, a dollar a ten o'clock scholar!" as we came in.

We took our seats as if everything were normal. As the day progressed, I raised my hand and told the teacher. "Our dad was in a bad accident this morning. He ran into a train. He's in the hospital, and he's in a coma. They don't know yet if he is going to make it."

It was all pretty matter-of-fact. I thought they had probably already heard it. I'm sure I was in shock. Finally, the teacher paid attention to these two traumatized girls in her classroom. We talked about it, answering questions and receiving reassurance from the other kids in the school. It was the best thing Ruth could have done, sending us to school.

Dad's injuries were very serious. He spent seven weeks in the hospital, and another year going to doctor appointments to fix his jaw and teeth so he could eat again. He came home to us a hundred pounds lighter, walking with crutches—truly a devastated man.

He made his way to the bedroom. We said "hello," but it didn't seem like our Dad. He didn't smile. He didn't seem glad to see us.

He took off his clothes and climbed into the bed. I wanted my Dad back, but he never came home again.

I had never known what depression looked like until then. Dad was so sad. I couldn't understand it. He had lived, hadn't he? Wasn't that more important than anything?

A gloom settled over the house. All of us walked on eggshells as Dad lay in the bed.

One day Mom called all of us together. We needed to go in and talk to Dad she said.

I took my place in the semi-circle with my brothers and sisters and Mom around the bed where my Dad lay crying.

"I think it would have been better for all of you if I had died. It just seems like I'm no good for anything anymore. I'm sorry you have to put up with me," the frail man spoke through his tears.

I didn't understand this. We were all crying. Mom told us we should tell Dad we were sorry that he hadn't thought that we were glad to have him back home with us. So, we did. One by one, we told him. "I'm sorry, Dad."

His work as a brick mason was a thing of the past. There was no money coming in. Mom had to drive him to his appointments. Lynn, Susie, and I were alone most of that year, it seemed, as my brothers earned money working for neighboring farmers to put food on our table.

Our oldest sister was away at college. Mom didn't want her to leave her studies.

It was fortunate that we had a basement filled with potatoes. We lived on potatoes and bread that year. Occasionally, someone from church would bring over food for us. Most of the time, food was pretty sparse.

The railroad had been negligent in not putting out flares that fateful day. Dad could have had a huge settlement, but he was not wanting more than he was entitled to have. His perception of the amount needed to raise all of us without his income was woefully underestimated. He took a meager settlement, and he and mom began to discuss options.

After much discussion, they settled on the purchase of a small, country store. Mom would operate the store. We would live above it. Dad could help my brothers run a tractor tire repair and other gas station service.

I walked out into the spring night with our dog, Laddy, at my side. This was a huge change for us all. We would be moving away from paradise. Our home in Albright's could have been purchased, but we needed a way for my parents to have an income.

I talked with Jesus about it all as we walked along outside. It seemed like I was in the middle of a dream. We would have a store. We would have a new home. We would go to town school.

I hated to leave Albright's, but it seemed like we were about to have a very great adventure. I thanked Jesus for what was to come. I needed Mom to be home again. Dad had been through an awful year, but he seemed to be better. Neither life nor Dad was ever going to be the same as it had been, but in my optimism, I saw only wonderful things ahead.

It is amazing how quickly life can take a complete direction turn. The very morning of the accident, Mom told us later, she had mailed off the last payment that she and Dad owed. She was so happy to be debt-free.

There is no way to prepare for being hit by a train, whether literally or figuratively. Those things that rock our security and make us understand that we have very little control over the lives we lead can be upsetting, and is, for many.

The reality is that we can't know what tomorrow holds. Even if we did know, we could not prevent it or even know the full impact that it would have. The circles of impact go out in every direction—just like the circles that go out from a pebble dropped into a quiet pool.

The rest and comfort that brings me peace is not because of what I have control over. It is because of who has control over me!

When the terrorists were crashing planes into the World Trade Center and Pentagon, when those courageous passengers were deciding to overtake the hijackers and crash the plane in an effort to save others, I was sitting blissfully unaware in a class at Seminary. We were not told of the tragic attack until we arrived at chapel at 10 a.m. CST.

Like the rest of the world, we were stunned. Chapel was cancelled. We went, instead, to spend time in prayer and in comfort of one another and the Lord.

It seemed impossible that we, the people of the most powerful country in the world, were under attack. What the next days, weeks, months, and even years held for us was uncertain.

My friend, Jan, and I began to meet with anyone interested, to pray for the terrorists. Surely, God who created them too, loved those misguided individual's plotting such horrendous acts even though they were acting in such unthinkable ways. We had no ability to do anything, except to pray.

It was so little, and yet, so much. Our prayers not only made our needs known before God, but also our prayers helped us to find solace and comfort as we began each prayer time in praise to God for his being—his power, his prevention of greater losses, and his ability to "arrest" the terrorist's hearts and change them.

Whether our concerns are about the entire world or our own personal world, it is important to acknowledge that we can't know and we don't need to know about the future. It is a great gift to have today, without a clue about what we might face tomorrow or fifteen minutes from now. Our ability to have peace comes from knowing who God is.

Victory

Words and music by Rita Weber
Copyright © 2001 by Rita Weber

When Jacob wrestled with the man until the break of day,
He came to see his struggle was with God.
That night deceitful Jacob was renamed "Israel".
His walk on earth would never be the same.

For he had victory in the midst of trial.
God came in suffering to give him strength for one more mile.
When he surrendered all his plans,
and placed his life into God's hands,
God gave him victory in the middle of the trial.

When Paul and Silas prayed and sang inside their prison cell,
A midnight earthquake loosed all who were bound.
Yet, none of them escaped there.
They all stayed in their place.
For in their hearts, true freedom they had found.

For they had victory in the midst of trial.
God came in suffering to give them strength for one more mile.
When they surrendered all their plans,
And placed their lives into God's hands,
God gave them victory in the middle of the trial.

When Jesus cried in agony in dark Gethsemane,
He cried to God, "Not my will, thine be done."
His gift of sweet surrender has paid the price for all.
His resurrection won our victory!

Now, we have victory in the midst of trial.
God comes in suffering to give us strength for one more mile.
When we surrender all our plans,
And place our lives into God's hands,
Then we have victory in the middle of the trial.
God gives us victory in the middle of the trial.

Loving God *Chapter 14*

God is a God of love. The Scripture tells us God is love. In fact, if we want to be in relationship with God, we must love one another. That is not always easy. It is safe to say that, in our own human capacity, it is impossible to love some people.

One of the most wonderful experiences I have had in my work as a counselor has been working as a facilitator for the Family Violence Project with groups of men who batter.

It was never my plan to work with that population. In fact, when I was in Social Work class, we had to write down the groups of people we would like to work with, and the ones we did not want to work with as clients. There at the top of my "Never Hope To Work With List" was "Men who are physically violent with their partners."

God's sense of humor or redevelopment plan for our souls is amazing. Whenever we say, "No, I will never do that!" you can plan that someplace along the line, we *will* be doing just that thing.

That was the case with these men. I didn't seek it out; the opportunity came and landed on my doorstep. I couldn't help taking the opportunity to observe the groups as an intern. I needed the hours of experience. But, later when an opening came up for a facilitator in our agency, the woman in charge of the groups said she wanted *me—only me*. I was pleased. By this time, I realized that my misperceptions about men who are engaged in physical assaults against their partners were nothing like I had imagined.

I began to do groups three times a week. I trained in other facilitators. I found myself doing work that amazed even me. I never knew what I did that worked, except that I truly loved those men. I know that the love I felt for them was not the usual love that we have as human beings for people we select to love because of characteristics we enjoy. This was a deeper compassion that God placed deep inside me. I didn't always like the individuals, but I always loved them.

Because I couldn't always see the expressions and body language of the group members, my co-facilitators would give me feedback after the group about things I couldn't know.

This was another situation where God used my blindness as a gift. These men were accustomed to intimidating by use of looks and non-verbal communications. This technique was totally wasted on me. I picked up on tones of voice and many times the things they said were overtly intended to intimidate me. It didn't work. God gave me a view of these men, most of them, as they were inside—broken little children who needed to experience love and respect they had never known in the past. Men who had never been made to feel that they were good and could act good. Men who always felt that they were losers.

God helped me to help them. As they developed a changed view of who they were, some of them had changed lives. Not all of them changed as a result of the group. I knew that. Yet, seeds were planted. They were given a chance to see the world differently. And, I always took consolation in the fact that, if they were not really changed, they would be back in the court system again, because they would be abusive again.

One of the things that we did as each man left the group was to give them feedback from each member in the group. I couldn't always think ahead of things to say, but as I spoke, the Spirit seemed to say things through me. Some of the men were visibly moved by what they heard, spoken in love. What happened to each of those men, I can never know. I do know this—I could do nothing to make a difference for them, but God could.

I am only responsible for making an effort to reach out to people and help them to see the possibilities. Beyond that it is up to them.

It isn't easy to create empathy for individuals who have been physically violent to other human beings. That is especially true in a world where there are notorious examples of arrogant, hate-filled individuals who have been seen in the media without evidence of remorse for their acts. Many times, there is only a sense that the person is sorry to have been caught and all the efforts put forth are in an attempt to beat the system.

Individuals who are sociopaths are not helped by domestic violence groups, and neither are individuals who have antisocial personality disorders. But, for those who fit the profile I share, the ones who are former victims, who truly want to change, for those individuals—group can work.

It is God's mission for us here on this earth to love God and love those who need our help—no matter how unloveable they are, each of us is going to have truth revealed some day when we stand before the Righteous Judge. What will he discover in you and me? Do we have a form of religion but fail to recognize the power of it? (II Timothy 3:5).

If only we could allow God's love to be revealed to us. If only we could truly bring what is needed to salt this earth and preserve it from corruption.

There was a song many years ago that went like this, "What the world needs now is love, sweet love." As Dusty Springfield sang those lyrics the truth of what she sang was evident. This world does need love, but not the kind the world promises and never delivers. The love we all need is the love that God has already given—free for the taking.

Sometimes I think it is because it is so simple that many people choose not to respond to the call of the Lord. Maybe if there were a manual, 2,543 pages in length, outlining all that we must do to be loved by God and to follow, that would bring in many people. Because then, the control would seem to be theirs in this matter. The Mosaic Law became such a thing for the people of the Old Testament which they tried (but failed) to follow. They could never obey the law to the letter, despite their best efforts. They always needed to have a sin offering given up for the sins of the people.

Jesus was asked about this law keeping. He told us that the entire law—all 600 plus of them, could be brought down to 2. We must love the Lord our God with all our heart, with all our soul and with all our mind, and we must love our neighbor as ourselves (Matthew 22:36). It seems too simple.

It is that simple. It is that hard.

As I sat at my computer one day, I accidentally pushed the "Control" plus the "R" keys. The text of the document I was working on all moved, immediately, to the right margin of the page. It still had all the typo's and poor grammar it had contained before. It was simply made to be on the right of the page. My screen-reading program announced, "Right justified."

I thought about what Paul says about being "justified by faith" in II Corinthians 5. Just like the text of that page, we are simply made right. It doesn't mean we are perfect. There are many things Christ needs to change in our lives. But when we have faith, God sees we have been justified. We are made right.

I noticed that the text had no power of its own to move to the right. That was not possible except by the one in control of the keyboard—me.

You and I might think we can make ourselves right with God, but we are dependent on the One who is in control. As long as we believe Jesus can justify us, we are justified by that faith in his power.

We are not perfect beings. We are only made right in the eyes of God as we put our faith in him. He is the only One who can bring about changes in our lives and in the lives of others.

That can be such a liberating thought. If I need changing, I need to let the Lord be free to change me. I cannot change myself. The Lord knows that I have tried. I can only be changed, just like the text of my document, as Christ changes me.

For the people around me, the same truth holds. We don't have to sit in judgment or try to manipulate people to change. We only need to pray for their lives to change by the power of the Holy Spirit's guidance. And, while we are down there on our knees, we can pray that God will change us to be more concerned about the log in our own eye (Matthew 7:3), and not the splinter in another's eye!

Jesus told the parable of the Good Samaritan in which a man goes out of his way to help a stranger in need in order to help us understand who is our neighbor we are called to love.. Do we love as Christ asked us to love? Or do we limit ourselves to the people who are easy to love?

Perhaps there are people you know who are in your life who you have a difficult time loving. You don't have to figure out how to love them. Just begin to pray for that one you struggle with, asking God's help in giving you his love. The Lord will change the feelings in your heart if you ask him to do it. Remember that God IS love. If you give love to another person, you are giving them GOD!

God loves us so much more than we can even think. And, why does he love us? Is it because we are so perfectly wonderful? No! The Scripture says that he died for us while we were still sinners (Romans 5:8).

Because God Loves Us

Before the world was formed
God had a plan to be with us.
Created in his image, we were made for fellowship divine.
But with the fall a chasm formed dividing God from us
—a chasm deep and wide that none could cross.

Because God loves us, Jesus came.
He brought salvation through his name.
Our great Redeemer,
He is Prophet, Priest, and King.
The Word, incarnate, came to earth
And brought the promise of rebirth.
Now with our Savior, we can live eternally.

Throughout this broken world
We see such pain and misery.
And, in our broken hearts we cry to God,
"Lord, why should this be?
How can a God with power to make
This glorious universe
Allow such suffering?
How can this be?"

Because God loves us, Jesus came.
He took our suffering, bore our shame.
He gave his lifeblood to redeem our weary souls.
He rose, victorious over death
—our source for hope, the Lord, himself.
For, over evil, Christ will speak the final word.

Only The Beginning

We were at war in Iraq. The soldiers were dressed in heavy uniforms for protection from the environmental hazards compounded by the incredible heat of the desert. They were away from kith and kin. Their strength and resources were of limited supply without continual reprovisioning deliveries.

It suddenly began to occur to me that our lives here are to be like those of the soldiers we were seeing on the 10 o'clock news. Even though they were living in another country, even though their work was involved in that land, they never quit being Americans. Their identity, their language, their future lay in the States, not in Iraq.

What if they had begun to talk like Iraqis? What if they had forgotten their homeland or the reason they were over there? What if they began to invest their time and energies in building a permanent home for themselves in this new place? What if they had forgotten the love and home that was still theirs, here in this land?

It seems that these things that are difficult to imagine happening are the reality for many of us who call ourselves "Christian." Although our home and our heart as members of God's Kingdom are held in heaven, we often forget, and take on the look and actions of one who is a citizen of this earth.

What is our mission anyway? Are we here only to live out our allotted years as best we can, judging our successes and failures by an earthly standard?

We are called to be light and salt in this world, Jesus said in Matthew 5. We who have been born again into this Kingdom are to carry the Light of Christ into the darkness in the world, not to join into it. Yet, how many times are we influenced by the way those who do not honor Christ operate? We watch the same television, we dress the same, we have the same worldly concerns, and we forget that we are not citizens of this earth!

As part of my reading in Theology class at North American Baptist Seminary, our professor Philip Thompson, required *Another City*[1] by Barry A. Harvey. This work challenged my thinking about being a

Christian. Did I live as a citizen of this earth or was I part of the King-dom of God, living in this "outpost of heaven" as Harvey put it.

The recognition that mainline denominations are filled with many nominal Christians had been troubling to me a long time. Now I was forced to look closely at my own life.

Another City was a difficult book to read. I read and reread, strug-gling to make sense of what was there.

I appreciated what was contained in the book that I was able to grasp, but my mind was feeling tired from two years of seminary. I was certain I wasn't able to fully take in all the book had to offer. It was only after I had written the paper and finished the class that its mes-sage began to work on my thoughts.

Jesus told the disciples that where their treasure is, there their hearts would be, too (Matthew 6:19-21). If we think about where our treasures are, it is a clear indicator of where our passions are engaged.

It isn't easy to be accountable for our thinking time and our ener-gies. It seems so normal to be preoccupied with family, career, invest-ments, and hedonistic pursuits. It is the normal and usual way most people think. Few in this world ever challenge that kind of prioritiza-tion.

Lest I leave the impression with you that I have had a straight and pious life all the way along, or that I am sitting in a place of judgment over others, allow me to say that I had a period of my life when I forgot where my citizenship existed. There was a time when I began to question everything about God.

It started when I was sitting in 11th grade English class. Our teach-er shared this quote with us, "Nothing is either right or wrong, but thinking makes it so."

That little statement began to work on my thoughts. I had grown up in the church. I had heard about Jesus and had practiced my faith in a sincere and certain way all my life. I knew that God existed, and he had done many important things in my life. Yet, I began to wonder— Did I only fool myself into believing that I was worshipping the way I did because it was right? Or, was it only because my parents had raised me this way that I believed it was true? I needed to know.

I prayed to God. "Please, God. I don't want you to leave me, but just give me a chance to know if what I believe is true, or if it is just what my parents said was true."

Looking back, I have great feelings of fear about what might have happened to me with such a request. It seems that what I was really asking was for God to give me permission to sin.

The years of my late teens brought about a serious change of lifestyle. I began to live a life that no longer had Jesus at the center of it. I may not have done things so wrong by worldly standards, but I was very far from God. By this time, I wasn't attending church. It was the first time I had lived away from home, and it felt good to just sleep in on weekends when I wasn't at work.

Karl, my future husband, lived in the apartment next door. He always went to church every Sunday. His church was not the one I grew up in. It seemed appealing to me that his church viewed the taboos that I had grown up with differently. It was possible to go out partying on Saturday night and have no guilt on Sunday morning. This was just what I needed, I thought.

In a few months, I talked with Karl about marriage. What if we would be married? How would our different faith backgrounds be worked out?

I agreed that I would join his church. I didn't fit into the strict church I had grown up with. I could worship God anywhere, I told him.

On the night we were married, my mother was not herself. She looked sick. She said very little. I knew it was hard on her and Dad to see me getting married in a church different than their own. Maybe that was what was wrong.

After the wedding, Karl and I drove several hours to a little vacation spot for our honeymoon. We had a nice hotel room. It seemed like the whole world was nearly perfect as we began our life together.

The next night, we went out for a fabulous dinner and then we found a place with a live band. It was such fun.

Over the loudspeaker, a voice paged "Karl Weber." We looked at each other. No one even knew where we were, did they?

"I told your brother, Curt, that we were coming here. I bet he called and told them we are on our honeymoon or something!" Karl guessed.

It was nothing like that. A policeman was waiting for us with a telephone number for a pastor and family friend.

"You need to give this number a call," the officer instructed.

My mother and father had been driving home from the wedding in Rochester when my mother became sick along the freeway in Minneapolis. They stopped along the edge of the road, where an officer stopped to see if they needed help. They were thinking they would get back on the road and drive home. Fortunately, the officer could tell that my mother did not have a normal flu bug. He took them to the nearest hospital where my mother was diagnosed with Acute Hemorrhagic Pancreatitis. Had they gone home, she would have died there.

By the time we called, she was in ICU. Twenty-four hours had passed with a steady decline in her condition. Despite my parent's desire not to interrupt our honeymoon, the doctor didn't think she would survive the night.

It was providential that Curt knew our destination. The police officer had driven around the area with a description of our car. Then he came in and brought us the emergency message.

Hours and miles drug by as we drove the six hours to the hospital. Mom was gravely ill. Even though she was in an excellent hospital, the doctors were pessimistic about her chances for survival. We were rushed into the ICU to see her. She was so filled with fluid in her abdomen, she could barely breathe. She lay there with labored breathing and tried to act normal. She was mentally confused.

It was several months before she recovered, with many set backs and emergencies that required unplanned trips to Minneapolis.

Karl admitted later, he had seen mom down in the basement of our new home the day of the wedding. He said she was very sick, but she asked him not to tell anyone. She hadn't wanted to ruin the wedding.

It was two weeks after nearly losing my mother that I was told I was going blind. What had seemed so perfect the night we wed had a very rocky start.

Throughout the next months and years, the struggles I had to face were very difficult. I needed the Lord more than I ever had needed him in my life. Yet, I felt such guilt. After all the bad things I had done, how could I ask God for his help?

I struggled on, feeling drawn to listen to preachers on a radio station I found. I began to listen to the 700 Club.

One day, Pat Robertson was talking about people who had drifted away from the Lord. He said that God was a forgiving God and invited me to call a counselor.

I called the number and prayed for God to forgive me. I couldn't believe it! Not only was God willing to take me back—he wanted to take me back. I was so grateful.

In Luke 7 there is a woman like me. She came in and washed Jesus feet with her tears and kissed his feet over and over again. A Pharisee questioned the situation. Didn't Jesus realize what a sinful woman this was who was at his feet?

Jesus told a parable. He spoke of two men, each of them owing amounts of money. One owed a large amount. The other owed a smaller amount. The one that they owed the money to forgave the debt of them both. Jesus questioned the Pharisee, asking which of the two would have more gratitude for the forgiven debt. The Pharisee acknowledged that it would be greater for the one forgiven for the larger debt. Jesus told him he was right.

Jesus explained that those who have been forgiven much are the ones who have great love for him. I am that person. I can never repay my debt of love to Jesus.

How I wish I had never strayed away. I was only shown love by Christ, and still I did so many things that must have hurt him.

There is nothing I can do to make up for those years. I only know that I am grateful that we have a God who is merciful. He is willing to forgive and to take us back when we have gotten off the path.

Last week, I had a dream just as I was waking up in the morning. I was a young girl, and before me was a lit stage, sitting amid the darkness of a large hall. Standing in position, all in full costume were the actors of the scene.

There were shepherds and wisemen, a few animals chewing and looking around. There stood Joseph and Mary before a small wooden manger of hay. It was all very big compared to me. I went up to the manger and stood up on my tiptoes to have a look inside.

"Oh, no! I heard the actors crying out. "He didn't come!"

The empty manger lay before me, but no baby was in sight. All the preparation and planning for the play was for nothing. The baby had never come.

I awoke with a sad and empty feeling—empty as that little manger had been. What an awful thought. What if Jesus had never come?

Yet, as I pondered that horrible notion, my thoughts were drawn deeper. What if Jesus hadn't come? Could God tell any difference in the way you and I live our lives? Do we act as a forgiven people who have a glorious hope in our Lord? Or, do we live no differently than if Jesus had never come? Do we go through a socialized ritualistic expression of religion, instead of having a genuine and life-changing experience of faith?

How our external demonstrations of religion must grieve our Lord when he sees a heart within us that has no genuine love for Christ. It is not possible to hide from God our true thoughts and motives in "worship" even if we can fool others and even ourselves.

What If

Words and music by Rita Weber
Copyright © 2004 by Rita Weber

What if God hadn't sent his only Son?
What if Jesus had decided not to come?
What if Christ had never shone his light
In this dark and sinful world?
Lord, I wonder. I wonder…

What if Jesus hadn't died upon the tree?
What if he had never shed his blood for me?
What if I was made to pay the debt I owe for all my sin?
Lord, I wonder. I wonder…

Refrain
Has Christ made a difference in the way I live my life?
Do I live as a citizen of earth, or of God's Kingdom?
Where do my treasures lie?
What has captured my heart?
When he looks at me, what does Jesus see?

What if Jesus hadn't risen from the dead?
What if he was held by this cold earth instead?
What if he had never conquered death
Or won the victory?
Lord, I wonder. I wonder…

To Refrain

What if Jesus wasn't sitting on God's throne?
What if we were forced to face this life alone?
What if Christ had never promised
He would come and take us home?
Lord, I wonder. I wonder…

Has Christ made a difference in my life?

A Walk of Faith

Whenever my husband and I go out into the world, I use him as my sighted guide. I may carry my cane, just for explanatory purposes, or to give me additional information about the terrain ahead, but primarily, I rely on Karl to guide me.

I hold his arm, just above the elbow, and position myself slightly to the side and behind him. His movements give me information to let me know if we are going up or down or squeezing between chairs—whatever I need to know.

I would never be able to do that if I didn't trust him. If I didn't believe he was watching out for me, that he loves me and won't let me come to harm, I couldn't follow him as I do.

Paul talks about "walking by faith, and not by sight" in II Corinthians 5:7. The verse has this same idea. I don't have the ability to see what is ahead and neither do any of us. But if we know whom we are holding on to as we walk, we know we can safely follow, wherever the path leads us. That is what blind faith is about. Recognition that we are able to travel safely when we allow the Lord to lead us is easier to say than to do. We sometimes see something that we think would be a better direction than where the Lord wants to take us. Unfortunately, we can't see the pitfalls as our Lord can. We are also unable to see the incredible possibilities.

A couple of years ago, my husband and I took a long weekend holiday to the Black Hills of South Dakota. The colors of fall were at their peak. We drove along, feeling fortunate to catch the beauty of this place.

Usually I see things in a general sense, from the small bit of vision I still have left. But, occasionally, the Lord gives me a chance to glimpse something in its full vision. This was such a day.

We drove around the curve of the highway, and there on the right was the most beautiful sight in the entire hills. The backdrop of the pine forest stood as a solid black background in my sight. There in front of the forest was a lovely golden yellow tree. It was so striking as it stood there against the dark hue of the forest. As I looked at it,

I began to think about how that gorgeous tree in all its glory is like some people.

Most of us are like the trees of the forest. We have a purpose to fulfill, and we are solid in the formation of this daily life. None of the individual trees have much distinction from the other trees. What gives them beauty is the whole of them, all standing there together.

But, occasionally there is a tree like this golden one that stands out in striking contrast to the rest of the forest. The tree itself was doing nothing to be glorious. It was only being what it was created to be. God had to prepare just the right level of moisture, the right temperatures, and all the right changes within the tree to make it possible for it to be so outstanding.

The tree was not filled with pride at its beauty. It was there, giving glory and pointing out the master works of its Creator. God was the one receiving glory, not the tree.

Those individuals who God intends to be made different from the rest of us stand out in sharp contrast—by their appearance, their talents, their intelligence. Whatever God intends in his wisdom becomes part of the special life he creates.

When we see a person like this in life, we are drawn to them. But, the truth is that they are only being who God made them to be. God alone creates just the right conditions to allow them to be so glorious. As we view these unique gifts on the landscape of life it is important to remember the tree. The person standing in such glory is not bringing glory to him/herself but to God.

Some individuals reading this are such specially created individuals. Because they stand out does not make them more valuable to God's world. He needs to have the forest of trees, as well, to fill their role. But our admiration and honor should not be to the person we find so special. It must be given to where it rightly belongs—to God, the Creator.

As we go through life, we can never know for certain what kind of tree we are to be. It is only in God's excellent plan fulfilled that each of us reaches our full potential. Our plans may not be nearly as glorious as God had in mind when he formed us in our mother's womb. That is the reason it is so crucial that we surrender to God's work in our lives. It is not about us. It never has been. It is always God's work—his creation, his circumstances, his perfect plan.

Just as those trees are important in impacting the ecological system of the world, you and I affect the overall ecology of the world, too. Whether intentionally or not, we have an impact for positive effect or negative. No one and no thing can exist without impacting the world. How we allow our presence to effect things is a matter of that same surrender to God's intentional work.

How we care for the environment, how we care for one another, is all part of being a follower of Christ. There is no one person more valuable than another among us. The needs and impact of each person on the globe is important in God's system.

When we focus our attention on doing Christian things–going to church on Sunday, saying important sounding prayers, oversee-ing the Christmas pageant–those things may seem to be evidences of holiness. What is it that the Scripture tells us about how our lives will be judged at the end of time? Is it about things that we in the institu-tional church view as signs of piety?

In Matthew 25:31 there is an important passage about the judging of the nations. Jesus speaks of the goats and the sheep being separated to his left and his right. What determines if one is a sheep or a goat? It is not how many offices you have held in the church or how many pews you have donated. It isn't even how many times you have sung a solo in the choir. The determination is based on what each has done in meeting the needs of others. Hunger, thirst, clothing, visitation of the sick and the people in prison are all listed as the work that we are to do, as unto Christ.

Yet, how much of our emphasis in our churches is about meet-ing those basic needs. We erect bigger and more beautiful edifices to house our congregations, while funding to reach out to those in need around us is being cut from the budget. You and I are influenced so much by what has become an institutional force that many times fails to meet the real needs of those in the community.

Walter Rauschenbusch[2] in the late 1800's took a call in a slum area of New York City. He was a gifted scholar, but when he saw the terrible living conditions of the people in the area, his heart was challenged. Jesus was shown, particularly in the gospel of Luke, Rauschenbusch thought, to be filled with compassion for those in need. He began to work at finding ways to provide for the basic necessities of life for the individuals in his congregation. It was the beginning of what has been called "Social Gospel."

Much has been done to criticize his work over the years. Meeting physical needs seemed to become detached from the good news of Jesus as the missing spiritual need filler.

As the debate continues of faith ministry versus social ministry, it seems that if Jesus were here today he would be doing both. He would be feeding the five thousand with bread and fish, but not without feeding their souls, too.

As I sat in class listening to Dr. Thompson share about the life of Walter Rauschenbusch, I heard him say that this social gospel was not a bad thing. It was only that it became the man's "sole focus." In my mind I heard this thought, "His ministry should have had a 'soul focus'."

Rauschenbusch allowed social needs to become his primary concern. Jesus used social-need-meeting to give him an opportunity to meet spiritual needs.

We are called to be about both in this world in which we live. It is not intended that we have a place where only those who act good enough and dress good enough are to come to worship God. Our churches need to go out into the highways and the hedgerows" (Luke 14:23) and have people come in to fill up God's house. Our churches were never intended to be social clubs where only those of a certain income bracket, educational level, or racial group are to be made welcome.

Blind faith is not just about following God's leading. It is also about being blind to the things that the world sees as important. Our ability to be blinded to the differences that divide and to see each other as God sees us is what we are called to be.

One day as I was preparing to give a sermon in my preaching class, I was praying for God's help. I was given a view of the class. It was not filled with men and women of varying shapes and sizes. Instead, in each chair there was a heart pumping. They all looked just alike. I couldn't tell gender or style of dress, or attractiveness level or intelligence or anything that we often use as criteria to determine our view of others.

God showed me that I need to minister to all people's hearts and not be caught up with who they are on the outside. Only God can truly see people's hearts. He alone knows if someone is committed to him or if the person is merely putting on a display for others to see.

As we come together to worship, we need to put on God's spiritual sight. We need to remember that the God who stretched out his arms in sacrifice for us is the same God who welcomes us all who are willing to come with sincerity.

We are not in church to be entertained or to be seen by others. We are invited into God's house. He warmly invites us to come near and spend time with him. His Holy Spirit, drawing us close, inspires our songs and our worship, helping us to feel the presence of the Almighty. Our worship is to be given to God, not to the person in the pew beside us.

It doesn't matter what style the music is that we sing. It matters that we are singing it with genuine hearts to our Lord.

Our God, who none of us has ever seen, who we must know only by the sharing of the Spirit, is worthy of that kind of worship. We sing and praise God because he is truly awesome, beyond what our poor, limited minds can grasp. He is the God who is without beginning or end, yet aware of the very number of the hairs on our heads.

God is worthy of our trust. He loves us with such pure love. His love is what is described for us in "the love chapter" (I Corinthians 13). Even though we may read that passage at wedding ceremonies and aspire to have that kind of love, God alone loves with that level of selflessness. How can we give any less to him than our love and praise?

A Psalm

Oh, Lord most holy, Ancient of Days,
We humbly bow our hearts and offer up this praise to you.
For you are Righteous, Faithful and true.
Maker of everything that is,
Our source of life is you.
For you are our fortress and strength,
Our help in times of trouble.
You have nestled us, safe, beneath the shelter of your wings.
Lord, you are our refuge,
The Rock on whom we trust.
You gently hold us
In the palm of your hand.
Our tongues will praise you.
Our mouths will declare your steadfast love.
Almighty God, how marvelous you are!

Trial Run

God didn't foist blindness upon me to be cruel. He allowed it, though. He knew the faulty gene that was part of my make-up. He saw me being formed in my mother's womb (Psalm 139:13). He let it be.

Am I angry with that? No, not any more.

My blindness has become a precious gift. It is because of my inability to see that I have found my hope in Christ. If I hadn't been born just like I am, I may not have needed to find God. I may have been too self-reliant, too certain in my own ability to discover all that I could never have done or known about without Christ in my life.

Suffering looks different for each of us. It is not a punishment, but a gift. It makes us God-reliant (II Corinthians 12:9) if we are also given the wisdom of the Spirit to look past our life experience on the earth to the future glory.

Jesus knows all about our suffering. He comes to us in it, if we ask him to come. He opens our eyes to see what we could never have seen otherwise.

"Otherwise"–it is great to be *otherwise*. God has given humans a certain amount of what we believe to be wise thought. It is only when we are challenged by the Holy Spirit in our earthly view of matters that we are given the opportunity to recognize that we are not really wise at all. Our view is too finite. Our thoughts are not God's thoughts. Our ways are not God's ways (Isaiah 55:8). We may want to be God-like in our thinking. The only way we can, though, is to allow God to transform our thoughts and our ways in accordance with his thoughts and ways.

This kind of transformed living is blind faith. It allows us to resist relying on our own perceptions. It allows us to see beyond what is humanly possible. It shows us where to look and gives us views of things that could never be seen by mere mortals.

One day, I will see it all with perfect clarity. Now I only see glimpses. Then I shall see Christ face to face and I will know it all perfectly, (I Corinthians 13:12). It will be wonderful, won't it?

Whatever our struggles and sufferings, whatever the cross we must bear to follow Christ, it will be worth it all. When we see Christ in his radiant glory, no tears will dim the eye then. Our searching hearts will be satisfied. We will look on glory greater than we can imagine. Paul tells us that we are being prepared to receive that weight of glory by our affliction here on earth.

I tried to understand what he meant by this "weight of glory." Then I remembered the Olympics. I watched the Awards Ceremony more attentively than any other part of the games, sitting up close to the TV screen. There each athlete stood up in front of everyone as the flag of the country he/she represented and the national anthem played in honor of the accomplishment attained.

Did you see what happened to the athletes? Their eyes filled with tears, their chests seemed like they would burst!

This was no ordinary moment. All the work and trials and disappointments each one had experienced on the way to this point in time were part of the present. Each had been preparing, not only physically, but mentally, emotionally, and spiritually to stand before the honor bestowed. Had they not gone through all that it took to come to this place, the significance of the honor, the weight of this glory would not have been felt.

Our life is filled with struggles. One day, like those athletes, we will stand before God and receive our own weight of glory. It will be all the sweeter because of the afflictions of this world. Until then, "Don't lose heart." God renews us every day, even though we may see evidences of our nature wasting away (II Corinthians 4:16).

Maybe the reason we get ourselves into trouble in this earthly struggle is that we spend too much time relying on what our earthly eyes are telling us. We look in mirrors and at pictures and we believe that those give the true picture of who we are. It is not so. God looks at our hearts. He sees us as we really are. That is the truth we must be more concerned about than the outside which appears to be who we are. If that is all stripped away, what does God see? Where is our focus fixed?

We need to choose. Do we wish to trust in our own perceptions? Or, do we willingly give ourselves over to trusting completely in God—no matter what we *think* we see. God is love. He is the only One in whom our trust is well placed. We can go forward without looking at what is around us, holding on to God, living by blind faith.

I Worship You

It is a mystery that God throughout history
Chose to reveal to us
Through his own Holy Word.
The Sovereign, Eternal One,
God—Father, Spirit, Son—
Who always was, and is, and ever more will be.

I worship you, for you are the Holy One.
I worship you, for you are the Lord.
You are the mighty King,
Creator of everything.
Father I worship you, because you are God.

Jesus, Anointed One, Only Begotten Son,
You spoke your Word and all creation came to be.
You are the Worthy Lamb,
Revealed as the Great I Am,
Our Prophet, Priest, and King who lives eternally.

I worship you, for you are the Holy One.
I worship you, for you are the Lord.
You are the mighty King,
Creator of everything.
Jesus I worship you, because you are God.

Oh, Spirit, draw us near.
It is your call we hear
That leads us into true devotion to you, Lord.
The Spirit has lifted us, encouraged and gifted us.
Forevermore, he will be worshipped and adored.

I worship you, for you are the Holy One.
I worship you, for you are the Lord.
You are the mighty King,
Creator of everything.
Spirit I worship you, because you are God.

Standing At The Edge

The late 1800's brought a flood of immigrants to this country. One among them was Gust Nivala. The son of a wealthy landowner who was a prominent man in Finland, the young man set his sights on the promise of his own success in America.

His father was adamantly opposed to the plan. Why go off to another country when he could go to University, study and prepare to take over the older man's agricultural empire one day? Why should there be any discussion? The older man was firm. "You go off to America and you will no longer be my son."

Gust was determined. Penniless, he found passage aboard a cattle boat. He left behind his father and mother, their large home and land holdings, the future inheritance, to come to this place and fulfill his own destiny. In spite of the price it would cost him in his relationships with those he loved, or future security, my grandfather came. There was no turning back. He knew that.

In C.S. Lewis's writings in *Miracles*,[3] he talks about the point in life when we must make a similar decision. It isn't about those earthly choices Gust dealt with. It is a decision about how we choose to view God.

Many times we wish to limit God. We can only feel comfortable if we are in control, if God is only a quantifiable force.

It is when we cross "the Rubicon" that we come to a place where we open ourselves to the miraculous workings of a limitless God. It is then that our lives can be far more than our own abilities, talents, and vision can imagine.

I sat across the table from my friend, Joan, while she finished reading the C.S. Lewis excerpt she had brought along to share with me. Then she asked my thoughts on what she had read. We talked a few moments, and then she asked, "Do you know what he means by crossing the Rubicon?"

"No. I don't know what 'the Rubicon' is," I replied honestly.

"I didn't know either, so I looked it up in a book. This is what it said."

Joan told me a story of Julius Caesar[4] who was a great orator and military man. He had manipulated his way to power and was very popular with the Celtics and Gauls he governed. Meanwhile, Pompey and the Senate became concerned about Julius Caesar's rise to power. They called on him to resign his post. In 49 B.C. he faced the choice: would he resign or face the risk of a bloody civil war? He and his men came through northern Italy to the edge of a small stream. He knew it was treason to cross that stream with a standing army. As he stood at the edge of it, he told his men that he did not know what they would face on the other side of that river. They may succeed or fail, but once they had crossed it there was no turning back.

Now, as we know from history, this was a pivotal event that brought about the rise of the Roman Empire, but when the decision was made on the bank of that stream there was no way to know it would turn out in that way.

You and I are called to cross into new territory. It is unclear what lies ahead, but if we make a decision to go, there is no turning back.

What is the Rubicon for you and me? That is only known by each of us individually. What lies on the other side, though, is that place where God is free to demonstrate his miraculous power. God is able to prove his incomprehensible and immeasurable ability.

Ephesians 3:20 says that God is able to do "abundantly far more" than we can think to ask. Just imagine that! Crossing the Rubicon has a price. It might change our earthly relationships or it may require that we give up our feelings of security. There must be a willingness to surrender control and allow what God will do to override any of our own plans or ideas. Maybe ours were too small anyway!

On the other side, the potential is beyond our comprehension. Just as the Roman Empire's expansion was greater than Julius Caesar might have imagined before he crossed the river, the territory that we may lay claim to is greater than our human thought can imagine. Not because of our own self, but by God's power!

It seems to me that "crossing the Rubicon," I told my friend, Joan, happened when I decided to follow God's call to go to seminary. I knew it was a risk, and I had every reason to fail!

My decision to attend meant a conflict with my husband, a huge debt, and a physical and mental challenge that was clearly beyond what was possible. I agonized over the decision more than any I have made in my lifetime. I knew that, once I went down that path, there was no turning back.

The decision was made, not because I wanted to make it, but because I felt that God wanted me to make it. I had to go ahead, in spite of all the human reasoning that said I shouldn't. I needed to trust that God was in this, and he would make it work. I had to surrender my control and say "Yes, Lord. I will go where you want me to go."

It isn't clear, even here on the other side of that bridge, what lies ahead. What will happen in my life, in my ministry, only God knows. He asks only that I trust his love and goodness. He will take care of the rest.

A few months ago, I was asked to sing one of my songs at my class's graduation party. The Scripture verse that had been selected as our class verse was from Philippians 4:17, "I can do all things through Christ who strengthens me."

I wanted to have a song that was about that verse, and a portion of the song came to me before that party. God had other plans, though. I sang a different song at the party. The next week the remaining part of the song became clear.

This verse had been another one that my mother had quoted to me often. She said once that it says in the KJV, "I can do all things through Christ which strengthens me." She told me that the word which could refer to the Christ, the source of the power. Or, "which' could refer to the situation. Once we have accomplished a task that is clearly beyond our own abilities, it gives us more strenth to take on the next challenge!

It made sense to me. The more we have evidence that Christ has been there to give us the ability to accomplish more than we can on our own, the more we are ready to take on even more.

Standing At The Edge

Words and music by Rita Weber
Copyright © 2004 by Rita Weber

Standing at the edge of the familiar,
About to step by faith into the great unknown,
How I long to know the future paths
The Lord has laid before me,
But the only things I see at all
Are the things already done.
As I look back at the places that I've been through,
I see the tears and the laughter,
Choices made along the way.
And, I'm reminded of the many times
That I knew that I would surely fail.
But, then I felt God's hand.
He was right there all along.

I can do all things through Christ.
I can go wherever he might lead me.
I can go through longest, darkest valleys
Or climb high to lofty mountain heights
For I know, whatever I must face
It is only by God's amazing grace
That I can do all things through Christ who strengthens me.

I can do all things through Christ.
I can go wherever he might lead me.
I can go through longest, darkest valleys,
Or climb high on lofty mountain heights.
For I know, whatever things in life I face
It is only because of my God's amazing grace
That I can do all things through Christ.
I can do all things through Jesus Christ, my Savior.
I can do all things through Christ
Who strengthens me.

Conclusion

This place across the Rubicon is about a different kind of thinking and being. Our ties are viewed in truth. We are no longer of this world. We are only here, serving at our King's pleasure, until he sees fit to allow us to return home to him.

So, the river is here once again. Whether crossing over the bridge at Albright's and following the leading of my brother, Gary, or taking the challenge to cross the Rubicon, this remains the same. We must have faith not in what we see with our eyes, but in who is leading.

I have searched for a picture of Jesus from the backside. If I want to truly be a follower, I need to keep my eyes on his back. He is the only one who needs to see the path ahead. If there is a danger ahead, or a choice in the pathway to be made, he will deal with it with far greater wisdom than you or I could have.

As children, we never knew where our brother was leading us. We only knew that he would not let us come to harm. He would be with us and help us if we needed him.

How much greater is our Savior's love for you and me. He knows what is good for us. He loves us far more than we can know in this life.

Fix your eyes on the Lord. Trust his willingness to stay with you and lead you. He will transform each of us into who he needs us to be—who he made us to be. God will make it all possible.

You Are Worthy, Lord

Words and music by Rita Weber
Copyright © 2002 by Rita Weber

Refrain
You are worthy, Lord.
You are worthy, Lord.
The hosts of heaven call you "Worthy".
You are worthy, Lord.
You are worthy, Lord.
By all creation, to be adored.

Though the essence of God, with Him an equal,
Yet, you emptied yourself
And chose to take the form of slave.
In humility you came by birth to live on earth as man.
In obedience, even to your death. (Death on a cross!)

To Refrain

Now exalted by God above the heavens
At the sound of your name
Every knee that is, will bow.
Every tongue will confess that you are
Jesus Christ the Lord.
You bring glory to your father, God.

To Refrain

Endnotes

---

[1] Harvey, Barry A. *Another City: An Ecclesiological Primer for a Post-Christian World*. Harrisburg, PA: Trinity House, 1999.

Freeman, Curtis W., James Wm. McClendon, Jr., and Rosalee Velloso da Silva. *Baptist Roots*. Valley Forge, PA: Judson Press, 1999.

[2] Lewis, C. S. *Miracles: A Preliminary Study*. New York: Macmillan, 1947, p. 114.

"So it is a sort of Rubicon. One goes across; or not. But if one does, there is no security against miracles.One may be in for anything."

[3]"Julius Caesar Crosses the Rubicon, 49 BC," *EyeWitness to History*, available at http://www.eyewitnesstohistory.com; Internet; accessed 2002.